LOVE IS
ALWAYS RIGHT

LOVE IS
ALWAYS RIGHT

A Defense of the One Moral Absolute

by
Josh McDowell & Norm Geisler

WORD PUBLISHING
Dallas•London•Vancouver•Melbourne

LOVE IS ALWAYS RIGHT

Unless otherwise indicated, Scripture quotations used in this book are from
the New American Standard Bible (NASB) © 1960, 1962, 1963, 1968,
1971, 1972, 1973, 1975, 1977 by
The Lockman Foundation. Used by permission.

Other scripture quotations are from the following sources:
The King James Version (KJV).
The New Century Version of the Bible (NCV),
copyright © 1987, 1988, 1991, Word Publishing.

Library of Congress Cataloging-in-Publication Data

McDowell, Josh.
    Love is always right / Josh McDowell and Norm Geisler.
    p.   cm.
    ISBN 0-8499-3965-8
    1. Christian ethics. I. Geisler, Norm L.   II. Title.

BJ1249.M275   1996   96-21867
241--dc20   CIP

Printed in the United States of America

6 7 8 9 QKP 9 8 7 6 5 4 3 2 1

CONTENTS

PREFACE

Ethics, particularly dilemma ethics, can be a controversial subject on which good Christian people have honest disagreement. My coauthor and I desire, however, to deal with these sometimes thorny issues of right and wrong from a *purely biblical basis.* Our foremost goal is to address some very difficult issues and use biblical principles as the framework for answering many gut-wrenching questions.

As you read this book, I would ask you to set aside any preconceived notions of what may be your right or wrong answer in the various situations examined. And, I ask you to approach each issue from a fresh perspective provided by principles gleaned from the Word of God.

While our intent is to be honest to biblical interpretation, you may disagree with our assumptions or conclusions. I welcome your response. Please feel free to write me and share your biblical concerns or comments. While I cannot promise to respond to each letter, I assure you I will carefully consider each concern you may express.

Norm Geisler
Box 471974
Charlotte, NC 28247

Josh McDowell
P. O. Box 1000Q
Dallas, TX 75221

ACKNOWLEDGMENTS

We would like to acknowledge the following people:

Ed Stewart for his expert writing skills in reworking the original manuscript and folding in the various new thoughts and materials from both authors.

Javier Elizondo and Edward Pauley for their professional and thorough critique of the completed manuscript. Their insights and clarifications were extremely helpful.

Dave Bellis, Josh McDowell's agent and associate of nineteen years, for guiding this writing project from beginning to end.

And finally, Joey Paul and Word Publishing, our publisher, for the encouragement and enthusiasm they have exhibited in bringing this work to print.

H omeless and hungry. Scrawled on cardboard with a crayon, the words grab your attention even before you stop for the light at the busy intersection. And you can't avoid seeing the man on the curb just outside your window, seemingly aiming the sign and his plaintive stare directly at you. His threadbare flannel shirt is a size too small. His jeans are ragged and soiled. His hair is greasy and unkempt, and his leathery face is shadowed by several days' growth. His eyes, which you try to avoid, seem empty from deprivation and neglect. He certainly looks homeless and hungry.

Your mind instantly floods with a familiar litany of responses, as if a committee of inner advisors are all shouting suggestions at once. And with every thought comes a protest from another side of your brain insisting why you should ignore such advice.

Do the loving thing. Give the poor guy that five

dollar bill in your wallet. No, don't give him money. He will probably take it straight to the liquor store and drink it down. He's just a panhandling wino hoping to sucker people with his homeless-and-hungry act. Your five dollars will go further toward helping the homeless and hungry at the local rescue mission.

Offer to take him to McDonald's for lunch or to the grocery store for some food. That's too dangerous. He may just be waiting for a gullible motorist like you to rob or kidnap. Besides, you have a full schedule today—no time for charity. Anyway, he could seriously stain your upholstery with his dirty clothes.

Hand him a tract and share Christ with him. Are you kidding? The last thing on this guy's mind is religion. If he's really homeless and hungry, he needs something to eat, and you can't help him there. If he's a phony begging money for booze or drugs, you *shouldn't* help him. Either way, he's not interested in a curbside sermon about heaven and hell.

The loving thing is to confront him about his laziness. Tell him to get a job and feed himself. But maybe he's not lazy. Maybe he's a good worker who is just down on his luck. By confronting him unfairly, you may make his bad situation even worse, and how loving is that?

After less than a minute—which seemed like half an hour—the light turns green and you drive on. Before you have traveled two blocks, your thoughts are back to your hectic schedule as if you had never seen the forlorn man with the cardboard sign.

◆

You are out the door and on the way to the hospital within minutes of hanging up the phone. Kathy, your next-door neighbor, just called in tears to tell you that Jarrod, the ten-year-old son of another neighbor, Alise, fell out of a tree and landed on his head. "His injuries are life threatening," Kathy had said, "and Alise is a basket case. She's a single mom with no family in town. Somebody should go sit with her." Your heart goes out to Alise, and you realize that you have an opportunity to share the love of Christ with her in this sudden, sad emergency. So off you go.

On the way to the hospital, your thoughts take a curious turn. *This wouldn't have happened, Alise, if you had kept better control of Jarrod. He is always trying crazy, dangerous stunts in his tree house or riding his bike carelessly or playing with power tools. And you just let him. That's why I seldom allow my son Michael to play at your house. Or maybe you were just too numbed by the alcohol. The whole neighborhood knows about your drinking. The bottles in the recycling bin at the curb each week tell the sad story. That's another reason why I don't let Michael come over. If you don't wake up, you may also lose your six-year-old daughter.*

By the time you reach the hospital, you have corralled your stray thoughts and turned your attention to caring for Alise the best you can. The volunteer at the information counter informs you that Jarrod is in surgery, and you know how bad Alise must feel. But when you walk into the waiting room, instead of falling into your supportive arms, Jarrod's distraught mother looks at you coldly. "Well, this is a surprise," she says, dabbing her eyes with a tissue. "I didn't think you holier-than-thou neighbors cared to be around the rest of us. You wouldn't let your kid come around Jarrod when he was healthy. Why are you showing up now that he's almost dead?"

You are stunned by Alise's words. You try to assure yourself that she is frantic with worry and not thinking clearly. But her icy glare and hostile words seem to drain the compassion right out of you. *Don't you realize that I took time out of my busy day to be here for you, Alise?* you respond silently. *I'm here to help you, not to judge you.* Part of you wants to look past her unkind words to the hurt behind them and ask how you can help. Another part of you wants to turn around and just walk away from your ungrateful neighbor. *Why are some people so hard to love?* you wonder.

◆

You guessed what the superintendent was going to say even before she opened her mouth. It was just a matter of time before she cornered you: "You've been attending Community Church now for about eight months, haven't you? I understand you did some teaching in your former church. Would you be willing to take over the third-grade class this fall? We're really short on experienced teachers."

You cringe inside. The last eight months in the new church have been heavenly—no responsibilities, no meetings, just show up for the services if and when you feel like it. You have tried to stay anonymous as long as possible while healing from a bad case of ministry burnout. God has put you back together again, but it feels so good not to be involved that you have put off all thoughts of volunteering for ministry. Now somebody has blown your cover, and you figure the Sunday school superintendent gazing at you expectantly won't take no for an answer.

What's worse, in your heart you know it's time to get back in the saddle. You have been a Christian for a long time, and you are well aware that the sidelines are only a place to rest for a while, not to retire to. You can't deny your gift of teaching or the satisfaction you have known in helping children understand and apply Bible truth to their lives. But neither can you forget the time commitment and hard work involved in teaching well, and you have never felt right doing less than your best. You know that saying yes to the superintendent will bring back both the joy and the stress of teaching.

Just a few more months off, Lord, you plead silently. *It feels so good to sleep a little longer on Sunday mornings. And I'm not looking forward to giving up several evenings a month for teachers' meetings, class social events, and one-on-one visitation with students. Can't you fix it so I can just show up on Sunday morning and teach the lesson and skip all the other stuff? Serving you can be such a pain sometimes. Will you lighten up on me a little this time? I love you, Lord, but does loving you always have to cost so much?*

GETTING ALONG

Perhaps none of the preceding scenarios describes your personal experience exactly, but you may identify with some of the elements in one or all of them. Even in the best of times, life seems to be a never-ending series of challenging situations, personal pressures, minor crises, and difficult decisions. And most of these tight squeezes involve people in some way. In fact, relationships are at the heart of many of our stresses and conflicts. We love our families, but spouses occasionally misunderstand each other and fail to fulfill expectations. Children in the home sap our energy and tax our patience with their demands for time and attention. Adult children drift away and aging parents meddle or require increasing attention and care.

The circle of relationships outside the home can be just as challenging. The atmosphere at work may be charged with competition among coworkers, demands from superiors, and disappointments from employees. Church leaders always seem to be urging us toward greater personal involvement in the ministry. Noisy neighbors bug us. Store clerks ignore us or foul up our orders. Teachers don't understand our children's needs. And everywhere we turn someone—the homeless, charities, church committees, the soccer league, and others—is in our face asking for something. We identify with one minister who quipped sardonically to another, "Being in the ministry would be great if it weren't for the people." And we sympathize with the harried homemaker who wondered, "Where does a mother go to resign?" We sometimes think life would be a lot easier without the people and the stressful challenges they present.

Even a personal relationship with God is not without its difficult moments. Obviously God is not uncaring, unfair, or overdemanding as some people are. But neither is He satisfied to be uninvolved with His people. He calls us into fellowship with Himself through worship and prayer. He encourages us to grow in His likeness through assimilating His Word and giving place to His indwelling Spirit. And He commands us to share the difference He makes in our lives with others. In reality, it is our association with the God who loves us that prevents us from disassociating with the people who bring most of the challenges into our lives.

Sometimes we consider ourselves ill-equipped for keeping in step with Christ and dealing with challenging people. We cry out to God when people pressures increase, "I can't hold up under the stress. I'm not people-proof." Yet God keeps putting us to the test by surrounding us with all kinds of people. God did not fashion us to be solitary islands. He custom designed us to interact with people of all kinds, even those who try our patience. None of us, even the most harried or introverted, can resign from being a people person. Getting along with people, helping people, working through difficulties with people, enjoying people, comforting people, and guiding people to Christ is what we are made for. Love requires an object. That's why God gave us one another.

A VITAL KEY FROM THE HANDBOOK

Thankfully, God did not design us for person-to-person ministry and then leave us without a clue as to how to do it. In His Word—the "manufacturer's handbook" for how we are to live out our designed purpose in the world—God has provided the master key for relating to Him and getting along with people of all kinds. The key is love, and God wrote the book on love, literally. From cover to cover, the Bible demonstrates God's love for His human creation; invites us to experience God's love personally through His beloved Son, Jesus; commands us to practice love at every level of relationship—human and divine; and provides instruction and example for the daily exercise of the Christian love ethic in our relationships. To love is to cooperate with God's unique design for His human creation and know the fulfillment that results from living God's way. Not to love is to miss the purpose for our existence and know little more than frustration and heartache in our dealings with people.

Love Is Always Right was written to help you better understand and more successfully apply this vital key in your daily interaction with God and people. Here's how the following chapters will approach the subject:

- Love is a universal moral absolute. To love is always right;

not to love is always wrong. Chapters 2 and 3 lay the foundation for the discussion of love by establishing the reality of moral absolutes and objective values in a world bent on moral relativism and subjectivity.

- Love is more than hearts, flowers, and dreamy songs. Love is conscious action and response. Chapters 4 through 6 tie a practical, workable definition of love to God's nature and contrast true love with popular misconceptions and caricatures.

- Love is not an option for the Christian. The supreme command of Scripture, as summarized by Jesus, is to love God and love people. Chapters 7 through 11 present the love imperative, delineate the various levels and responsibilities of love, and anchor love in God's law and Christ's exemplary life.

- Love is often difficult. Sometimes the responsibilities of love overlap and conflict, making it hard for us to choose the loving thing. Chapters 12 through 14 explore love in conflict and provide value principles for exercising love when moral dilemmas cloud our vision.

- Love never fails, but sometimes we fail at loving God and others. Despite our best intentions, we occasionally do the unloving thing. Chapter 15 provides helpful guidelines for returning to center when we fail to love as we should and when others fail to love us as they should.

- Love has an infinite number of applications. It is impossible to anticipate every question about how love responds in various relationships, situations, and conflicts. But we have tried to anticipate several such questions. Each of the chapters closes with a section of "tough questions and straight answers" in which some of the more difficult applications of love are considered.

What difference can love really make? For Sid and Lani, the love of strangers spelled the difference between life and death. Their "love story" is true.

One Friday morning in the spring of 1970, a young hippie couple from the big city showed up on the doorstep of a little country church. Sid and Lani had been living together for two years, and Lani was six months pregnant. "We want to get married as soon as possible," they told the minister in his study. The minister was rather indignant at this interruption by bedraggled flower children who regarded his nice church as little more than a roadside wedding chapel. Hoping that a delay would discourage them, he said, "If you will attend church on Sunday, I will marry you after the morning service." The minister was confident that he would never see them again.

But on Sunday morning, the minister looked out to see the couple in the congregation, quite the sight in their long hair and ragged bell-bottoms. When the sanctuary was nearly empty, Sid and Lani met the minister at the altar for a simple ceremony. When congregation members realized that a wedding was about to take place, about thirty people hurried back into the church, happy to participate in the festivities of the strangers. "Why are they here?" Lani asked, bewildered. The minister said, "I guess they just care about you."

After the brief ceremony, Mildred, one of the women in the congregation, stood and asked the couple, "Where are you two going for your honeymoon?" Mildred and Jack had celebrated their twenty-fifth wedding anniversary only days earlier.

"I don't know," Sid said with a shrug, "maybe up into the mountains to camp."

"Well, first you need dinner and a wedding cake," she announced with a warm smile. "You are coming to our house for dinner. In fact, everyone is invited to our house for dinner." While the minister busied the couple signing certificates, Mildred hastily organized a potluck. When the couple and the minister arrived at Mildred's home twenty minutes later, the table was spread with sandwiches and salads. In the center of the table was the top layer of Mildred and Jack's anniversary cake.

The celebration went on for six hours. Lunch and cake were consumed, and the bride and groom were cheered and congratulated. They left that evening beaming at the heartfelt hospitality of the small congregation.

Two and a half decades later, a middle-aged couple drove up to the same little country church. They explained to the current minister that they had been married in the sanctuary twenty-five years earlier and engulfed by the loving congregation on their wedding day.

The minister had never heard the story, but a woman working in the office overheard the conversation. "I remember you," she said to the couple. "I was here that day and attended your wedding. Mildred is still in town. You must come to lunch with us."

Sitting at the table with the two elderly women, Sid and Lani told their story. The first eleven years of their marriage had been disastrous. Sid was on drugs and Lani was an alcoholic. One day, with their lives on the verge of collapse, Sid said, "We have been to church only once in our lives: the day we were married. It was a good experience for us. Maybe we should go again." They attended a church near their home, gave their lives to Christ, and were transformed. "It's our twenty-fifth anniversary," Sid told the women, "and we just had to return to the little church that means so much to us."

Today Sid and Lani are Christian drug counselors in the city. They freely admit that it was the love and acceptance of a congregation of farm folk for a couple of dirty hippies that ultimately turned their lives around and saved their marriage.

All around us there are people like Sid and Lani in need of genuine, transforming love. Each of us has the opportunity to be a Mildred to such people every day. May the following pages inspire and equip you to spawn an ever-expanding anthology of love stories among the people with whom you come in contact.

WHAT'S WRONG—OR RIGHT— WITH THIS PICTURE?

2

Chad walked into Denny's office at four o'clock, exactly when his supervisor had asked him to be there for the brief meeting. An up-and-coming hardware designer at ComCraft Corporation, Chad suspected that he had been called in for another positive "attaboy" session. Denny was good at acknowledging his employees for their successes, and over the past four years, hardworking Chad had given his boss plenty of reasons to praise him.

Denny was on the phone, so he motioned Chad to shut the door and sit down. Slipping into an upholstered chair near the desk, Chad regarded his boss with a gaze of appreciation. Denny was not only a good boss, but he was also becoming a friend. The two men had attended a few ball games together, and Chad planned to invite Denny and Barb to church when the time was right. Chad hadn't brought matters of faith into their relationship yet, but he hoped to soon. The prospect of working for a *Christian* boss some day excited him.

Denny wrapped up his conversation and switched off the phone. He pinched the bridge of his nose as if battling a major headache. He didn't look happy. Chad waited. Finally, Denny spoke. "I've been instructed by personnel to sign us up for a class."

Chad and his boss had attended a number of professional conferences and seminars together at ComCraft's expense. They always had fun, usually finding time for at least one round of golf. But Denny clearly wasn't enthused about this one.

"What class? Where?" Chad probed.

Denny blew a long sigh and pinched the bridge of his nose again. "Bertelli says you have to take a unit of sensitivity training, and I have to go with you," he said, avoiding eye contact.

Chad cocked his head, suddenly perplexed. "Sensitivity training? Me?"

Denny nodded slowly.

"I don't get it, Denny. Sensitivity training is for employees who aren't fitting in—hotheads, bigots, guys who harass their secretaries. What's the deal?"

Denny still wouldn't look Chad in the eye. "Do you remember a conversation you had about two weeks ago with Bob Romano from Precision Silicon Parts?"

"Which conversation?" Chad responded with a little laugh. "I talk to Bob Romano two or three times a week—his office, my office, on the phone. PSP is one of my prime suppliers. How could I remember one conversation?"

"I'm talking about a specific conversation," Denny pressed, finally looking at Chad, "the one where you and Romano discussed his . . . alternative lifestyle."

Chad's eyes popped wide open. "How did you hear about that?"

Denny ignored the question. "Did you tell Romano that you don't approve of his homosexuality?"

Chad blinked hard, shocked at the question. "Where are you coming from? What's this all about?"

Denny held up a sheaf of papers, a lengthy memo from personnel. Then he asked again. "I need to know, Chad. Did you or did you not tell Romano that you disapproved of his homosexuality?"

Chad lifted his palms in a gesture of innocence. "Bob happened to mention that day that he was gay, which I had already figured out. We talked about it for a while, then I said something like, 'I accept you as a person, and I enjoy working with you. But I don't agree with the homosexual lifestyle.' I didn't call him a queer or a faggot or anything—I would never do that. I just stated my opinion about his lifestyle. Does somebody have a problem with that?"

Denny leaned back in his executive chair and gazed at the ceiling tiles. "Yeah, somebody has a problem with that. Romano reported it to his boss at PSP and—"

"*Reported* it?" Chad interrupted, raising his voice. "It sounds like you're talking about a crime. We were just having a conversation, and I simply expressed my opinion. Bob didn't seem upset at all."

Denny held up his hand, signaling Chad to let him go on. "The brass at PSP called Evans upstairs, Evans called Bertelli in personnel, and I got this memo."

"And the memo says . . . ?"

"The memo says that you are required to attend a sensitivity training class. And since you're on my team, and I apparently didn't tutor you sufficiently about tolerance, I have to go with you."

Chad sat up straight. "Tolerance?" he snapped, obviously irritated. "What do you mean, tolerance? I'm one of the most tolerant people you'll ever meet. I'm a Christian. I accept all people equally, even those who are different from me, even Bob Romano."

"But you don't approve of his lifestyle," Denny inserted.

"Of course not," Chad said. "Homosexuality is a deviant lifestyle."

"According to whom?"

"The Bible says it's wrong, pure and simple. And common sense says it's abnormal. You know, male and female anatomy . . . "

Denny shook his head slowly. "That's intolerance. You can't say that, especially in the workplace. That's why you have to do this sensitivity class, which, incidentally, will be taught by a lesbian."

"A lesbian?" Chad whined incredulously. "I can't believe it!" Then he stood and began pacing the large office. "Where did you and personnel get your definition of tolerance, anyway?"

"Right out of the company's new policy manual. Haven't you read it?"

Chad looked away. "Well, er, it's in a file in my office."

"Bertelli quotes a section in his memo," Denny said. Then he read aloud: "'ComCraft ownership and management affirm that all values, beliefs, and lifestyles of its employees, vendors, and customers are equal and exempt from challenge. Any ComCraft employee exhibiting attitudes of discrimination or intolerance toward other employees, vendors, or customers will be subject to disciplinary action or dismissal.'"

Chad stopped pacing. "Does that mean I could be fired simply for expressing my beliefs?"

"No, it means you could be fired for claiming or inferring that your beliefs are more credible than someone else's."

Chad spread his hands again to plead his case. "All I said was that I don't agree with Bob Romano's lifestyle."

Denny leaned forward in his chair, picked up a pencil, and pointed the eraser end at his coworker. "You can't do that, Chad," he said with a firmness Chad had rarely seen in his boss. "It's 'politically incorrect,' as they say. It's a put-down. It makes people feel different, inferior, oppressed. We need to celebrate diversity, praise the uniqueness of others."

"I can't believe what I'm hearing," Chad said, shaking his head. "It's not good enough for me to accept Bob Romano as a person; I have to praise him for being gay, even though I believe homosexuality is wrong?"

Denny nodded authoritatively.

Chad exploded. "That's ridiculous!"

"No, that's tolerance," Denny said, bouncing the pencil once on its eraser for emphasis.

"Well, I think it's crazy," Chad argued. "What you call tolerance is wiping out the lines between right and wrong."

"Wait a minute," Denny inserted, sounding irritated himself. "Who made you Christians the authority about what's right and wrong for everybody?"

"It's not just Christians. Certain things are right, and certain things are wrong. It's always been that way. Homosexuality is wrong. Abortion is wrong. Euthanasia—"

Denny sprang to his feet and angrily interrupted. "What right do you have to tell me that Barbara's abortion was wrong? The fetus was brain damaged; amniocentesis proved it. We spared that child a short, painful, meaningless life, and we saved ourselves from the prolonged suffering such a life would bring. Nobody can tell me what's right for me—not you and not your fundamentalist subculture. I determine right and wrong for myself. For one, I'm glad to see that society is waking up to the dehumanizing intolerance of Judeo-Christian values."

Chad stood speechless for several seconds. Then he said, "So you agree with the policy manual and with personnel's decision about me and Bob Romano?"

"One hundred percent. It's the way things are, Chad. And if you can't go with the flow on this, your career at ComCraft may be shorter than you planned."

CHOOSING SIDES OVER RIGHT AND WRONG

The preceding story is fiction. But if Chad's encounter with Denny sounds too bizarre to be true, you may be in for a shock. If you don't think serious clashes of values like this are being played out daily in business, government, education, and relationships, you are living in a dream world. If you assume that right and wrong are as clearly black and white to everyone else as they seem to you, you're naive. If you believe that the conscience of the Western world is still guided by objective truth, honesty, moral purity, and the Golden Rule, you need to take a closer look at how the people around you are living. And if your Christian values have not been challenged or ridiculed as archaic or irrelevant by a neighbor, coworker, teacher, or student, either your lamp is under a basket or the people you interact with day by day are blind and deaf.

Times have changed. Until the 1960s, America was predominantly Christian. Church attendance was socially acceptable. Belief in God and the Bible was widespread. Public prayer occurred at football games, school commencements, and city council meetings. Judeo-Christian values were considered right; opposing values were considered wrong.

Then about three decades ago, we transitioned into what the late Christian thinker Dr. Francis Schaeffer termed the "post-Christian era." The non-Christian population grew apathetic toward the church, the claims of the Bible, and the social values derived from them. Church attendance declined, but Christians were still tolerated by the defectors. "The Genesis creation is a myth, the resurrection of Christ is a fable, and the Christian lifestyle is a crutch for weak-minded people," they declared. "You Christians can believe that stuff if you want to, but don't push it on us, because we don't buy it anymore."

The world's live-and-let-live attitude toward Christians and their values continued through the 1970s and 1980s. But in the last decade of the twentieth century, we have reached a new low. American society has entered a period that may well be called the "anti-Christian era." As illustrated by Chad's encounter with Denny, apathy toward Christians and their beliefs is turning to antagonism. Issue conflict is moving from content to style. It's not *what* we believe that upsets non-Christians today. We are under attack for considering our beliefs and values to be universal and for failing to accept the values and lifestyle choices of others, even when they are in conflict with Scripture. The world angrily demands, as Denny did of his subordinate, "Who made you Christians the authority about what's right and wrong for everybody?"

At the core of the conflict are moral absolutes, because absolutes form the basis for what is right and wrong. Yet not everyone accepts the existence of absolutes today, and some who accept them do not believe they are universally applicable, as Chad found out during his heated exchange with Denny.

What is your experience? Do you have difficulty accepting the reality of moral absolutes in life? Is everything in flux, relative to the moment, to the situation, or to the people involved?

Or are there eternal constants that govern human experience and guide your choices? Can a behavior be right for one person and wrong for another? Can a behavior that was wrong at one time or in one situation be right at another? Is it appropriate to use words like *never* and *always* when discussing right and wrong? These questions and their answers are critical to the Christian's survival in an increasingly anti-Christian culture. And they are vital to establishing the foundation for the Christian love ethic presented in the following chapters.

IT'S ABSOLUTELY IMPOSSIBLE TO DENY ABSOLUTES

Skepticism regarding absolutes is not a recent phenomenon. About 500 years before Christ, the Greek philosopher Heraclitus theorized, "No one steps into the same river twice, for fresh waters are always upon him." He argued that everything is in flux: Nothing is permanent and abiding; nothing is changeless except change itself. Heraclitus's successor, Cratylus, took the argument a step further. He contended that no one steps into the same river once. There is no essence or substance to life at all, just movement. When asked if he existed, Cratylus simply wiggled his finger, indicating that he too was in a state of constant flux.

In more recent times, two influences have lent support to the view that we live in a moral vacuum with no absolutes. Anthropologists have concluded that very few, if any, human behaviors are judged to be wrong by all people everywhere. Stealing, lying, cheating, and infidelity are considered wrong by most cultures, but exceptions have been observed and reported. Even long-standing traditional moral taboos, such as killing and incest, are considered right by some tribes. Scarcely anything believed to be wrong by one group of people is not just as strongly believed to be right by another group. Add to this apparent cultural relativism the scientific relativity of time and space propounded by Albert Einstein, and it's easy to understand why people today are opposed to the idea of universal absolutes.

Denying that any behavior is absolutely right or wrong in itself is also evident in the widespread acceptance of situation ethics, popularized by Joseph Fletcher in the 1970s. To Fletcher, morality was not static but relative to each situation. He taught his disciples, "In every moral situation, do the loving thing." Sounds wonderful, doesn't it? Yet in Fletcher's mind, the loving thing was not absolute but relative. He explained that in some situations, adultery is the loving response and stealing is the higher good. Even killing may be justified in certain circumstances, according to Fletcher. No action is intrinsically and absolutely right or wrong for all persons at all times in all circumstances. Personal morality is more like wet clay than marble; it is subject to being molded and shaped to fit each occasion.

Much of today's society, in harmony with anthropological findings and situation ethics, agrees that no moral absolutes exist to govern human behavior. Yet there is a subtle and telling inconsistency in such denial. There is no way to deny absolutes without utilizing an absolute. It's like saying, "Never use the word *never*," or "It's always wrong to say *always*." When someone insists that no absolutes exist, he or she unwittingly admits to at least one! In reality, there is no way to avoid absolutes.

Even Heraclitus acknowledged that there was an unchanging law—which he called *logos*—beneath the constant flux of life. Einstein recognized that all things cannot be relative. He posited absolute Spirit (God) to which everything else is relative. After all, it doesn't make sense to say that A is relative to B and C is relative to D unless there is a standard to which A, B, C, and D are all relative. Absolute change is no more possible than lifting the earth in space with a board and fulcrum. Even change is impossible unless there is an unchanging base in relation to which the change can be measured.

The dilemma of the relativist may be illustrated by one of the Winnie the Pooh stories. Winnie the lovable bear has a notorious appetite, which brings him to the door of Rabbit for something to eat. When Winnie the Pooh knocks, Rabbit, who has no intention of feeding the bear, calls out, "Nobody home." Wise Winnie responds, "There must be somebody home or else he could not say, 'Nobody home.'"

Winnie is right, of course. Rabbit cannot deny his own presence unless he is present to deny it. Similarly, those who deny the existence of absolutes cannot hold that all things are relative unless there is some unchangeable ground on which their affirmation can stand. It's senseless to pronounce everything relative while not allowing that very position to be relative as well. In reality, the relativist stands on the pinnacle of his or her own absolute in order to pronounce everything else relative.

THE TRUTH ABOUT ABSOLUTE TRUTH

Chad stated confidently to his boss, "Certain things are right, and certain things are wrong. It's always been that way." But what are those "certain things"? Once we admit, as we must, that absolutes exist, where do we look for them? Who or what determines right from wrong? Are there alternate standards for different cultures, different times, and different locations? Is the belief in absolute truth a subjective opinion or an objective standard? If you haven't grappled with these questions, you will as our culture continues to shift away from absolutes and accepted Christian values. And if you haven't yet fallen into a dialogue or argument with non-Christians similar to the one between Chad and Denny, your time is coming, especially if you espouse a belief in absolutes.

We will respond to these basic core questions only briefly. If you are interested in digging deeper into the subject, we recommend *Right from Wrong* by Josh McDowell and Bob Hostetler. Another helpful book on the topic is *Christian Ethics* by Norm Geisler.

Absolute Truth Is Objective, Not Subjective

During the Vietnam War, I (Josh McDowell) was interviewed by a female reporter from the *Boston Globe* following a free speech rally. She was very vocal against war and killing, so I decided to play the devil's advocate in order to find out where her convictions were based.

"What's the problem with killing?" I asked her.

"Killing is wrong," the reporter insisted.

I pressed on. "Why is it wrong?"

"Because it's just wrong," she said, sounding frustrated that I would question the obvious.

I kept the pressure on. "Who told you that?"

"My parents taught me that war and killing are wrong."

"And where did your parents learn about the so-called evils of war and killing?"

"From their parents," she answered. "My family has always believed that war is wrong."

I got right in her face. "Do you mean to tell me that it's wrong for me to go to war because that's what your grandparents taught your parents and your parents taught *you*? What about people who were taught that war and killing are just and right? What about Nazi parents who taught their children that killing Jews was right? If war is really wrong, wouldn't it be wrong in all cultures?"

The reporter had no answer. Her strong conviction had a weak foundation: subjective opinion instead of an objective standard. When right and wrong are subjectively determined, one person's idea of morality is as good as another's. Human reasoning, conditioning, and emotions will lead some people to believe an act to be wrong while others are just as convinced it is right. Without external guidelines for behavior, people can talk themselves into believing almost anything as right or wrong.

Absolute truth is an objective standard, something outside ourselves. Right and wrong aren't items we accept on the strength of a majority vote, nor do they rise and fall with what people think or feel is right at the time. The fundamental moral and ethical guidelines proceeding from absolute truth must stand independent of personal opinion.

Absolute Truth Is Universal, Not Limited

When something is absolutely right, it is right for all people in all places under all conditions. Absolute truth does not change from person to person or from place to place. If something is considered right for one culture but pronounced wrong for another culture, it would not be absolute. If some people are judged right for a certain act while others are judged wrong, it would not be absolute. If it's right in some situations and wrong in others, it would not be absolute. If it's right in this country but wrong in that country, it is not absolute. Moral guidelines cannot be altered to fit certain cultures or geographic locales.

Rather, people and places must change to accommodate what is absolutely right and wrong.

Absolute Truth Is Constant, Not Changing

Right and wrong is timeless. Right *was* right in the past, *is* right in the present, and *will be* right in the future. It doesn't change from day to day, from year to year, from decade to decade, or from century to century. Right and wrong do not alter with the seasons or change to stay in fashion. Truth remains constant and dependable.

ABSOLUTE TRUTH PERSONIFIED

Where do we find absolute moral and ethical guidelines that are right for all people, for all times, and for all places? The following paragraphs from *Right from Wrong* bring us to the heart of the answer:

> It is impossible to arrive at an objective, universal, and constant standard of truth and morality without bringing God onto the stage. If an objective standard of truth and morality exists, it cannot be the product of the human mind (or it will not be objective); it must be the product of another Mind. If a constant and unchanging truth exists, it must reach beyond human timelines (or it would not be constant); it must be eternal. If a universal rule of right and wrong exists, it must transcend individual experience (or it will not be universal); it must be above us all. Yet, absolute truth must be something—or Someone—that is common to all humanity, to all creation.

> Those things—those requirements for a standard of truth and morality—are found only in one person—God. God is the Source of all truth. "He is the Rock," Moses said, "his work is

perfect . . . a God of truth and without iniquity, just and right is he" (Deut. 32:4, KJV). You see, it is God's nature and character that defines truth. He defines what is right for all people, for all times, for all places. . . . Truth is objective because God exists outside ourselves; it is universal because God is above all; it is constant because God is eternal. Absolute truth is absolute because it originates from the original.[1]

Absolute truth is not primarily an ideology or a heartless moral code. Absolute truth is first and foremost a person. The basis of everything we call moral and good and right is the eternal God who created us. Truth isn't something He decides; truth is something He is. For Jesus said, "I am . . . truth" (John 14:6). Particular attitudes and actions are right because they reflect God's nature. Conversely, attitudes and actions that conflict with God's nature are wrong.

For example, everyone has an inner sense of what is fair or unfair because the God who created us is a just God. Love is cherished and hatred scorned because God is a God of love. Honesty is right and deceit is wrong because God is righteous and true. Sexual purity is right and promiscuity is wrong because God is pure and holy. Whenever we choose to believe or act in harmony with God's nature, we have chosen what is true and right. Whenever we choose to get involved with something that is opposed to God's nature, we have chosen what is false and wrong.

There is another way to look at the issues of truth and right and wrong as they apply to the critical, rubber-meets-the-road areas of daily Christian living and relationships. What would you give for a master key that unlocks the right response in every moral dilemma you face? In the Scriptures, God has given us such a key: love. Love is the overarching guideline, flowing from God's nature, that helps us determine right from wrong on a practical, daily level. In the next chapter we will explore this marvelous key to making the right choice in any and every situation.

TOUGH QUESTIONS AND STRAIGHT ANSWERS ABOUT ABSOLUTE TRUTH

What about people who don't believe in God or the Bible? How can we convince them to accept God as the source of absolute truth?

First, reason with them. All legislation has a legislator. There can't be an absolute moral law without an absolute Moral Law Giver, and that's God. If they need a more detailed explanation, direct them to *Mere Christianity* by C. S. Lewis, the former Oxford atheist.

Second, live the truth. You have to live what is right if you want people to believe what is right. If your unbelieving family members, friends, fellow students, coworkers, and neighbors can't see love and right behavior in action in your life, if they can't see a difference in how you handle life's difficulties and dilemmas, they won't buy into it. For example, you can talk all you want about the importance of integrity and honesty. But if you cut corners or shade the truth in your business deals, you will drive your coworkers and customers away from God as the source of truth instead of drawing them near. If you cheat on school exams or your income tax or have your kids tell telephone callers you're out when you're in, you can't expect your family members to embrace the truth. If absolute values are not manifest in your daily experience, you'll never convince others to receive them into their lives.

Third, challenge them to be honest and open, to read the Bible anyway and give it a chance. The Word is powerful (Heb. 4:12), and God can work through it even when they don't believe it.

I think I know what's best for me. Why should I look for absolute values outside my own knowledge and experience? Why are objective values superior to subjective values?

Subjective values is an oxymoron—a conflict of terms. *Subjective* refers to the small circle of one individual's personal understanding, experience, or feelings. *Values* cannot be cornered by one individual. As we have demonstrated in this chapter, right and wrong exist independent of personal opinion. Ultimate values are outside us, above us, and beyond us. We do not judge what's true by how we think, feel, and act; we judge how we think, feel, and act by what's right and true. Moral values are not *determined* by us, they are merely *discovered* by us.

What is the role of conscience in determining what's right?

Conscience does play a role in helping us discern right from wrong, but it's not the role we often ascribe to it. The human conscience is an internal guidance system installed by God at creation to provide us with a basic sense of right and wrong. But the conscience can be conditioned and reshaped by how we respond to what is right. Paul indicated the frailty of the conscience when he wrote, "My conscience is clear, but that does not make me innocent" (1 Cor. 4:4). Some people have a "seared" conscience (1 Tim. 4:2), unable to clearly determine right from wrong. Nevertheless, God has revealed His moral law to all people. Indeed, it is written on our hearts (Rom. 2:15).

Ideally, as individuals seek God and open themselves to His Word over the years, their consciences are shaped by His truth, equipping them for making right choices. Individuals living together form cultures, and Western culture was originally conditioned by the Judeo-Christian values taught in the Scriptures. But individuals and cultures can experience a seared or dulled conscience by ignoring the truth or purposely choosing what's wrong. That's why the United States has moved from the Christian era to the post-Christian era to the anti-Christian era.

We have allowed our national and individual consciences to be dulled through pride and worldly pursuits. On many issues we have our values turned upside down. Right is wrong and wrong is right. Take abortion, for example. Hundreds of thousands of women in America believe it is right to terminate the life of an unborn child. The internal guidance system originally programmed against murder has been shorted out through self-centeredness and greed. A dulled conscience is more of a hindrance than a help in discerning right from wrong.

The only way your conscience can help you in discerning right from wrong is by allowing it to be molded by God's absolute moral law, which is written in our hearts and in His Word. Of course, the best way to be molded by God's law is to continually expose your heart and mind to the truth of the Bible. Only as the conscience is properly informed will it work for you instead of against you in your pursuit of truth.

IT'S ALWAYS THE RIGHT THING TO DO

3

Mr. Benson, the new teacher for the seventh-grade boys Sunday school class, decided that his first lesson would be on the will of God. After teaching his heart out for forty-five minutes, he concluded the lesson with an application question: "How can we know God's will for our lives today?" Most of his students studied their shoes or doodled on their worksheets in silence as they had throughout the class. But one boy with a confident grin eagerly shot up his hand.

"Yes, Donny," Mr. Benson said expectantly.

"I think the best way to find God's will is to read the Bible and pray," Donny said with assurance.

"Right on, Donny!" Mr. Benson exclaimed. The teacher went home that day rejoicing that he had gotten through to at least one of his students.

The following Sunday, Mr. Benson taught about temptation, concluding, "What's the best way for Christians to recognize temptation and say no to it?" Nobody seemed to have paid attention during the lesson, but again Donny's hand was up.

"Mr. Benson, if we read the Bible and pray every day, we won't give in to temptation."

Mr. Benson beamed with delight. "Thank you, Donny. You're right again." The teacher left the class elated at his success.

The topic for the third week was faith. "How can we grow in our faith?" the teacher concluded, eyeing his star pupil. Donny didn't disappoint him.

"Read the Bible and pray, Mr. Benson; that's how faith grows."

Mr. Benson quietly assured himself that after only three weeks he was probably the most successful Sunday school teacher in the church.

After class, Mr. Benson pulled Donny aside. "I just want to thank you, Donny, for paying attention to the lesson and answering the key questions."

"Oh, I don't pay attention in class," Donny responded with bald-faced seventh-grade honesty. "I'm thinking about my baseball card collection and soccer scores just like all the other guys."

The teacher's expression twisted into something resembling a question mark. "But you always come up with a thoughtful answer to my questions. You must be hearing something."

"Mr. Benson, I've been in Sunday school since I was a baby," Donny replied. "The only thing I know is that 'read the Bible and pray' is *always* the right answer."

Do you sometimes wish that life was as uncomplicated for you as Sunday school was for Donny? Wouldn't it be great if, in all our dealings, deliberations, and difficulties with people, there was always one right answer, one right thing to do that worked every time? We don't mean to oversimplify such a vital issue, but there really *is* a universal right thing to do that is applicable and appropriate in all our relationships. Love is that right answer. Love is always the right thing to do. Both culture and Scripture attest that all moral absolutes can be reduced to one: To love is always right; not to love is always wrong.

AND THEN THERE WAS ONE

In *Mere Christianity*, C. S. Lewis names several moral principles that have no known exceptions in history. For example, no culture anywhere has ever held that cruelty to children or rape is right. Though many cultures condone war and capital punishment, no civilization has ever believed it is right to kill indiscriminately any person for any or no reason. Nor has any culture approved of a man taking any woman he wanted at any time. There have always been limits on human relationships and behaviors, even in non-Christian cultures. Furthermore, Lewis argues that moral principles are very similar from people to people.

This similarity has prompted a number of thinkers to attempt to reduce all common moral principles to one basic moral absolute, one foundational right thing to do. German philosopher Immanuel Kant identified this absolute moral principle as the "categorical imperative," an unconditional duty binding on all people. The categorical imperative is one of morality. The right thing is what you could will everyone to do under the same circumstances. In short, it is something you can universalize for everyone.

The way to discover this prime duty, Kant said, is to ask concerning each action, "Do I want the guideline behind my action to become a universal law?" If the answer is no, then that action is wrong. Take lying, for example. We should not lie, Kant would say, because if lying were universal, there would be no more truth to lie about, and then lying would be impossible. Universal lying would be self-defeating. Likewise, murder is self-defeating and wrong. If murder were a universal law, eventually—hypothetically—there would be no more people to murder.

Kant also claimed that taking out a loan without means or intention to repay it violates the categorical imperative. If everyone followed this practice, the whole institution of human promises would collapse. He further deduced that it is immoral for those of means to refuse help to those suffering hardship. Otherwise, should you fall on hard times, Kant said, you could not be helped.

At the heart of Kant's categorical imperative is an irreducible moral law: *Always treat people as an end in themselves, never as only a means.* There are innumerable ways in which we treat others as means to personal ends. Some are selfish, but many are not. You go to the bank and a teller completes a financial transaction for you. At the market a clerk scans your grocery purchases, and a clerk's helper bags your order. You attend the symphony where dozens of people you don't know personally entertain you with beautiful music. Suspecting a prowler in your neighborhood, you call a policeman, who makes sure your home is safe. Even in these encounters with nameless, faceless providers of services, says Kant, we must treat people as ends, as valuable in *themselves*, not merely as means. We must act with courtesy, respect, affection, admiration, or any of the countless attitudes we call love.

Martin Buber, a twentieth-century Jewish philosopher, also held as a moral absolute that people should be treated as ends and not only as means. We must sustain a person-to-person relationship with others, not a person-to-thing relationship. Buber termed it "I–You" versus "I–It." Your boss is not a paycheck dispenser, a machine you must coddle or coax or kiss up to for personal financial security. Your boss is a person who is in need of understanding and love. Your employees are not stepping stones to your success; they are people who also have families, goals, and dreams. The income tax auditor is not a money-grabbing monster but a person who needs recognition, friendship, and affirmation, just as you do. Persons are to be loved, and things are to be used. We should never use people and love things. Buber asserted that I–You is a universal norm for human behavior to which there should be no exceptions.

A RULE FOR THE AGES

You don't have to be a philosopher or theologian to realize that Kant's categorical imperative and Buber's I–You resemble the age-old principle known popularly as the Golden Rule. Jesus said, "Do to others as you would have them do to you" (Luke 6:31). It is important to note that in the context of this statement Jesus was instructing about love, especially love for those we are least likely to love. "Love your enemies, do good to those who hate you, bless those who curse you, pray for those who mistreat you. . . . If you love those who love you, what credit is that to you? Even 'sinners' love those who love them. . . . But love your enemies, do good to them, and lend to them without expecting to get anything back" (Luke 6:27, 28, 32, 35). Clearly, murdering, deceiving, and using other people are not love because no one wants to be treated that way. Snubbing people contemptuously, gossiping about others, cursing at a motorist for a driving mistake, or shortchanging a difficult customer do not reflect love because we wouldn't appreciate such treatment. The Golden Rule is the great love mandate of the Bible, the essence of the Christian love ethic.

There is only one viable candidate for the overarching, irreducible moral absolute, the all-time right thing to do. It is a guideline that encircles Kant's categorical imperative, Buber's I–You concept, and other attempts at summarizing the essence of moral behavior. Simply stated, *we must always love.* Love is what allows us to treat others as ends instead of means. The ultimate test of morality is, "Did I act in a loving way?" Love is not a manifestation of the Golden Rule; the Golden Rule is a manifestation of love. To love is always the right thing to do. Furthermore, love is an absolute without exceptions. It applies to all people at all times in all places. Jesus answered, "'Love the Lord your God with all your heart, all your soul, and all your mind.' This is the first and most important command. And the second command is like the first: 'Love your neighbor as you love yourself.'" (Matt. 22: 37–39 NCV).

While there are no exceptions to the moral imperative to love, there are certainly alternatives, such as indifference and hate. However, these alternatives prove to be self-defeating. Even people who practice indifference and hate object when others treat them indifferently or hatefully. In other words, we may somehow feel justified in snubbing others or spreading rumors about them or calling them names. But if they do anything like that to us, we feel wronged whether we have provoked those actions or not.

Furthermore, if everyone practiced indifference and/or hate, meaningful human relationships would be completely nullified. Such actions not only fail the test of the Golden Rule but also violate Kant's categorical imperative and Buber's I–You. Love is the only moral absolute that is not self-defeating. Everyone wants to be loved, so everyone must love.

Love is also the only moral absolute that is universally recognized. Notice that we did not say universally *practiced*. Morality is not determined by what people *do* but by what they *ought* to do. You cannot always determine what people believe they ought to do by observing what they do. For example, you may believe wholeheartedly that you ought to love your neighbor, but do you practice that belief? Often, perhaps, but surely not always, and probably not often enough to satisfy even yourself.

Therefore, it is a mistake to judge a person's moral beliefs by his or her actual behavior. A convicted serial killer on death row may agree that murder is wrong. A man who cheats on his income tax or a woman who lies about her age may admit that honesty and truthfulness are virtues everyone should practice. You may be strongly in favor of law and order and still violate the speed limit every time you drive the freeway. Moral behavior reveals only what a person *does*, not necessarily what he or she thinks *ought* to be done.

"If we can't determine a person's moral beliefs from behavior, how can it be done?" you may ask. There are two ways.

First, you can tell what people believe is the right thing to do by what they say is the right thing to do. We have already noted that the great creeds and moral statements of history are very similar and reducible to the absolute of love. C. S. Lewis wrote an entire book on the subject. In *The Abolition of Man*, Lewis reports on numerous moral codes that he studied in the world's great cultures. Remarkably, these moral codes closely resemble the second table of the Ten Commandments, God's directions for relating to others. People across cultural lines will state that the moral principles embodied in the Ten Commandments and the Golden Rule are the basic code of human relationships. When you ask people how they ought to live, they will usually come up with the right answer: Do to others as you would have them do to you.

Even most non-Christians will say that love is essential. Kant's categorical imperative and Buber's I–You are in harmony with the Golden Rule. Bertrand Russell, famed for his book *Why I Am Not a Christian*, later wrote, "What the world needs is Christian love or compassion." Noted psychoanalyst Erich Fromm declared that lack of love is at the root of all psychological problems. Confucius had the same basic principle although it was stated negatively: Do not do unto others what you do not want them to do unto you. Basically, moralists have said the same thing through the years about what is absolutely right and wrong: To love is right and not to love is wrong.

Second, you can determine what people believe they ought to do by what they *expect others* to do to them. The most fundamental test of the morality of a course of action is rooted in a person's own moral expectations. It's not how an individual treats others but *how an individual wishes to be treated by others* that reveals what he or she really believes is right. More fundamental than either moral actions or moral expressions are moral expectations. The universal expectation to be treated decently and fairly is the most glaring evidence that love is the one irreducible moral absolute.

One of Norm Geisler's former students, who now teaches philosophy, introduced this reality to one of his students in an eye-opening way. The teacher assigned his ethics students a paper to write, but they were free to choose their own topics.

One brilliant young man chose to defend his personal view that there are no moral absolutes, that everything is relative. After reading the well-written, well-documented paper, the teacher marked it with an F and added, "I don't like blue folders."

After receiving the disappointing grade, the student stormed into the teacher's office. "What was wrong with my paper?" he demanded.

"There was nothing wrong with your paper," the teacher explained calmly. "In fact, it was very well done."

"Then why did you give me a failing grade?" the student fumed.

"Because you put your paper in a blue folder, and I don't like blue folders," said the teacher.

"That's not fair! That's not right! You should have graded me on the content of my paper, not the color of the folder!"

The teacher responded, "Didn't you claim in your paper that moral views are a matter of taste or opinion, such as some people liking chocolate and others liking vanilla?"

"Yes," the student agreed.

"Well," the teacher said, "I don't like blue, so you get an F."

Suddenly, the light went on for the young man. He realized he was trapped in his own argument. His expectation to be treated fairly revealed a belief in ethical absolutes he had previously been unwilling to acknowledge.

Let's put this theory to the test in a couple of scenarios closer to home.

You're in the right-hand lane of a four-lane highway in heavy traffic. A sign announces that the left lane is closed ahead and instructs motorists to merge right. You allow one car to slide in ahead of you, but then you ride its bumper to keep other cars from slipping in, especially the lead-foot driver in a red

Camaro who raced up the vacated left lane, hoping to cut in just before plowing into the orange highway cones.

He should have merged twenty cars back when he first saw the sign, you think smugly to yourself as the guy motions in vain for you to let him in. The Camaro finally noses in behind you—after flattening a couple of orange cones. When the left lane opens up again, he roars past you with an icy glare.

A few miles down the highway, your lane is closed. The cars in front of you dutifully slow and merge left. Ordinarily, you would too. But you're heading for an appointment, and you have a chance to gain some time by speeding up and ducking into line in front of a truck or a slow driver. It's an important appointment, so you go for it.

Half a mile later, as you approach the orange cones, you look for your spot, but it's not there. The left lane is bunched bumper to bumper, and nobody is ready to let you in. You flip on your blinker and wait patiently for a kind soul to make room for you. "Come on, people, let's be fair about this," you mutter. Surely they understand that you're in a hurry and that you don't usually do this. You're not a speed demon like the guy in the red Camaro—who also cruises by without letting you in. You sit there in front of the orange cones steaming at the insensitive drivers.

What do you really believe ought to happen in such situations? Even though you were not the most charitable of drivers when others needed to merge in front of you, you obviously believe the right thing to do is to let people into your lane when they request it. You proved your moral code through what you said about fairness and through your expectations, as demonstrated by your angry reaction to the drivers who shut you out. Your expectations tipped off your true beliefs. Loving in this situation means allowing other drivers to cut into traffic ahead of you—even lead-foots in red Camaros—because you expect drivers to cut you some slack when you need to merge.

◆

Consider another setting. During your annual performance review, you pressure your supervisor strongly for the maximum cost-of-living and merit increases allowed. You itemize your many accomplishments during the year and refer to industry standards for your position. The company hasn't done as well as everyone had hoped this year, but you have done your part, and you deserve to be rewarded accordingly.

You also sit on the church board to determine the pastor's annual salary increase. The budget is tight again this year, and some programs are being cut. You would like to vote the pastor a good raise, but other programs will suffer if you do. You rationalize that he is a servant and can supplement his income by performing weddings and funerals. So you suggest a small increase and promise to pray faithfully that God will supply all his needs.

What do you believe is the right thing to do for a good employee? You obviously believe that employees ought to be rewarded well for their efforts because that is what you expect from your employer. To follow the Golden Rule in the case of your pastor means applying your moral belief to his situation. Or it means changing your belief and sacrificing financially for your employer as you ask your pastor to do.

What we expect others to do for us and our loved ones is the key to our real moral beliefs. As Jesus said, what you want others to do to you is the basis for what you ought to do to them. Our morality is to be judged by what we say is right and expect to be done to us. For with our mouths we say what should be done and in our hearts we know what we expect others to do to us.

DO THE ONLY RIGHT THING

Is love really the ultimate moral absolute, transcending lines of culture and even faith? The answer is seen in human experience.

First, simple observation of human nature indicates that all people everywhere hope and expect to be loved. Everyone wants to be treated with fairness, respect, courtesy, and honesty. People who are mentally and emotionally stable are not happy when they are assaulted, abused, slandered, lied to, cheated, robbed, belittled, or ignored. Rather, when treated in an unloving manner, most people react negatively. They become angry, distraught, disillusioned, or hurt, revealing that the unloving treatment was an unwelcome intrusion rather than a cherished expectation. People universally act as if they deserve the respect and dignity inherent in love, so it is right to love.

Second, think about yourself. Don't you generally hope for positive, loving treatment in all your relationships and encounters with others? And don't your negative emotions kick in when you fail to receive the treatment you expect? For example, don't you expect your spouse and children to appreciate what you do for them, as evidenced by your disappointment or hurt when they take you for granted? Don't you expect store clerks to serve you quickly and courteously, as evidenced by your indignation when they regard you as an interruption in their lives? Don't you expect your boss to be sensitive to your needs, as evidenced by your frustration when he or she seems preoccupied with higher profits, lower costs, and more customers?

It seems safe to conclude that all people expect to be loved and therefore ought to love others. Refusing or failing to love others either denies that they are persons or reveals us to be inconsistent with our own moral expectations. The Golden Rule simply summarizes what human behavior and personal expectations convincingly witness. Since we expect to be loved, we ought to love others. To deny love to others is to deny their personhood. And if all people call for love, then love cannot be consistently limited only to some people or to one person— yourself. If you acknowledge that you hope for and expect loving treatment from others, then your expectation demands that you also love others.

Jesus was asked by a lawyer hoping to trap Him in inconsistency: "Who is my neighbor?" (Luke 10:29). Jesus answered with the parable of the Good Samaritan, who risked his own safety and expended his time, effort, and resources to aid a Jew who had been beaten and left for dead. The parable indicates that any person whose need we are able to meet should be considered our neighbor. More broadly, a neighbor is anyone who is in need of love. Love is the irreducible moral absolute. Love is always the neighborly thing to do. Go and show love to all.

TOUGH QUESTIONS AND STRAIGHT ANSWERS ABOUT
THE GOLDEN RULE

Can unbelievers really obey the Golden Rule without knowing God, the source of love?

Yes, because you don't have to be a Christian to live out biblical truth. In fact, sometimes the Golden Rule is followed more faithfully by unbelievers than by some Christians! Unbelievers can live out the Golden Rule without knowing that God is its source simply because, even to people in a fallen condition, treating others as you would like to be treated makes sense. As illustrated by Immanuel Kant and Martin Buber, love appears to be a universal moral absolute quite apart from a personal knowledge of God or relationship with Jesus Christ.

However, as kind and loving as he or she may be, every unbeliever must understand that salvation comes through faith in Christ alone, not through following the Golden Rule. People must be led from the commonsense nature of loving others to the scriptural principle of love and to the person of God Himself, the source of love.

How does the Holy Spirit fit into the Christian love ethic?

The Holy Spirit is essential to living out the Christian love ethic. Many people, including unbelievers, can follow the Golden Rule on sheer willpower with a high degree of success. But to actually *live* the love ethic day in and day out requires supernatural power from within, the Holy Spirit's power. The difference is especially discernible when the heat is on, when loving is most difficult. People who are negative, abrasive, or hateful challenge our human determination to treat others as we want to be treated. The natural, fleshly response is to act in kind. It's in these situations that we need the Holy Spirit's supernatural ability to love. Also, when we become tired, stressed out, or peopled out, our willingness to be loving may wear thin. We need power beyond ourselves to follow through with what we know is right.

The Holy Spirit is indispensable to our success at doing the loving thing when we don't feel like it. Even a car with no engine can roll down hill. It's when life is an uphill battle that we realize we need the power of the Spirit to love as we should (Rom. 8:3, 4).

What's the difference between the Christian love ethic and just following our conscience and common sense?

Conscience and common sense may be generally reliable, but they are also fallible. The human conscience, though it may be disposed to some degree to do the right thing, can be conditioned by worldly influences, fleshly desires, and the devil's temptations. Common sense implies widespread social acceptability, and public opinion can be skewed by the same negative forces that affect personal conscience. Without an objective standard for behavior—specifically, a moral absolute anchored to God Himself and expressed in His moral law—eventually you will be off the mark.

YOU DON'T KNOW LOVE
IF YOU DON'T KNOW GOD

4

In *Mortal Lessons: Notes on the Art of Surgery,* Dr. Richard Selzer tells of his encounter with a young woman after he removed a tumor from her face. Surgery required the severing of a facial nerve, leaving one side of her mouth lifeless and crooked. The surgeon was concerned about how the woman and her husband would respond to her new appearance.

Her husband is in the room. He stands on the opposite side of the bed, and together, they seem to dwell in the evening lamplight. Isolated from me, private. Who are they, I ask myself, he and this wry-mouth I have made, who gaze at each other, and touch each other generously, greedily?

The young woman speaks. "Will I always be like this?" she asks. "Yes," I say. "It is because the nerve was cut." She nods and is silent. But the young man smiles. "I like it," he says. "It's kind of cute."

All at once I know who he is, I understand, and I lower my gaze. One is not bold in an encounter with a god. Unmindful, he bends to kiss her crooked mouth, and I am so close I can see how he twists his own lips to accommodate hers, to show that their kiss still works. I remember that the gods appeared in ancient Greece as mortals, and I hold my breath and let the wonder in.[1]

As Dr. Selzer suggests, love is a godlike quality. But we are not gods. Love is something human beings need and express, but love is not our basic nature. It is something we *have*, not something we *are*. Love resides within us and operates through us by the presence of the Holy Spirit, but its source is beyond us. Since love is an absolute, it never changes. Therefore the ultimate source of love must be as changeless as love itself. As Christians, we identify our changeless God as the source of love. The Bible states clearly: "God is love" (1 John 4:16). In contrast to His human creation, God does not *have* love, He *is* love. God's activity of love flows from His nature of love. When God loves, He is simply being Himself.

No meaningful love ethic can avoid the knowledge of the God of love who is revealed in Scripture. The command to love means nothing unless we know what love is, and the meaning of love is rooted in God. John wrote, "Whoever does not love does not know God, because God is love" (1 John 4:8). The Christian love ethic is no more secure than its source and no more applicable to life than our knowledge of His law.

How do we gain this knowledge of God's love? There are two basic sources: the world around us and the Scriptures. Our experience of God's love in creation and human relationships is a general source of knowledge about Him. The Bible is a more specific source. We will consider both.

SURROUNDED BY GOD'S LOVING NATURE

The spring rain falls gently on your tiny backyard vegetable garden. Raindrops bead on the leaves and the green fruit of healthy tomato, zucchini, lettuce, and carrot plants that promise a tasty summer harvest. You can't get over it. Just a few weeks earlier there was nothing here but dirt. You planted the seeds, watered them, then watched day by day. The warm spring sunlight coaxed green sprouts from the moist earth. Almost before your eyes the tiny seeds had produced a bounty of beautiful vegetables, enough to feed your family with plenty to share with the neighbors. You think about farmers who grow food by the hundreds of acres and make a good living at it. You think about poor people in Third World countries who grow what little they can just to survive. You wonder if they are also in awe of the miracle of seed, rain, sun, and harvest.

Our experience of living in this world informs us that there is a God who cares about the earth He created and the creatures who live upon it. As Paul preached to the unbelievers at Lystra, God "has not left himself without testimony: He has shown kindness by giving you rain from heaven and crops in their seasons; he provides you with plenty of food and fills your hearts with joy" (Acts 14:17). The psalmist said of God, "You open your hand and satisfy the desires of every living thing" (Ps. 145:16). God promised Noah, "As long as the earth endures, seedtime and harvest, cold and heat, summer and winter, day and night will never cease" (Gen. 8:22). The earth's abundant and timely fruitfulness, its pleasing blend of symmetry and contrast, its breathtaking sensory beauty, and its intricate design—from the macrocosm of space to the microcosm of the subparticle realm—is a witness of God's love in keeping His promise through the millennia.

Paul spoke of our utter dependence on the loving Creator, reminding the non-Christian philosophers on Mars Hill that God "is not served by human hands, as if he needed anything, because he himself gives all men life and breath and everything else" (Acts 17:25). The witness of nature is sufficient to convince every human being of the existence and provision of a God who made us and cares for our needs. Paul wrote, "Since the creation of the world God's invisible qualities—his eternal power and divine nature—have been clearly seen, being understood from what has been made, so that men are without excuse" (Rom. 1:20). Nature is a constant and unclouded testimony to the existence of a God of love.

Our knowledge of God's love in the world around us is not limited to what we generally call nature. God has also revealed His love to us through the love of His human creation. The apostle John declared, "Love comes from God. Everyone who loves has been born of God and knows God" (1 John 4:7). The tender love of parent and child, the selfless, intimate love of husband and wife, and the enduring, committed love of lifetime friends are evidences that the God who created us is a God of love. Every time someone runs errands for a shut-in, provides meals for a sick friend, donates money or materials for disaster relief, helps a neighbor move furniture, or performs some other loving deed, God's love is reflected in human behavior. As Christians, we know we are the instruments of God's love to others, for "Christ's love compels us" (2 Cor. 5:14). Love is from God, and those who experience true love, whether believers or not, sense there is a God who cares.

Obviously, love is distorted in our world. Sin and sickness in the hearts of humankind have twisted human love into pride, hatred, and vengeance. Strife, envy, and bitterness have separated individuals, families, races, socioeconomic groups, and nations. And yet human love is universal. All cultures have some regard for decency and respect in human relationships, as demonstrated in their civil laws and moral codes. For example, Attila's Huns may have been savage in their hatred and destruction of their enemies, but they loved their own spouses, children, and friends. Except perhaps for the most heinous, deranged, or diabolical of criminals, we would be hard-pressed to find one individual in the world who did not love someone: a parent, a sibling, a mentor, a spouse. And even the faintest glimmer of love in the human heart evidences the imprint of the loving God who created us.

THE FINAL WORD ON THE GOD OF LOVE

The most explicit knowledge of God's love is derived from the Bible. In literally hundreds of references in both Testaments we are told of God's love. Some entire chapters, such as 1 Corinthians 13—called "the love chapter"—are devoted to love. Love is the dominant theme in books such as Hosea, the gospel of John, and John's first epistle. According to Jesus, love is the overall theme of Scripture. He said, "'Love the Lord your God with all your heart and with all your soul and with all your mind.' This is the first and greatest commandment. And the second is like it: 'Love your neighbor as yourself.' All the Law and the Prophets hang on these two commandments" (Matt. 22:37–40).

In the Old Testament, the Law (the first five books) and the Prophets (the last seventeen books, Matt. 5:17; Luke 24:27) summarize God's instruction about how to live in loving relationship with Him and others. The outworking of these relationships is chronicled in the books of history and celebrated in the books of poetry. When Jesus said "All the Law and the Prophets," He indicated that God's love permeates the Old Testament. Even in the midst of delivering the Ten Commandments, God declared that He is committed to "showing love to a thousand generations of those who love me and keep my commandments" (Exod. 20:6). The psalmist interjects the phrase repeatedly, "His love endures forever" (Ps. 136:1f).

Also repeated throughout the Old Testament is a rich and descriptive phrase of the loving nature of God as He revealed Himself to Moses: "The Lord, the compassionate and gracious God, slow to anger, abounding in love and faithfulness, maintaining love to thousands, and forgiving wickedness, rebellion and sin" (Exod. 34:6, 7; see also Num. 14:18; Neh. 9:17; Ps. 86:15, 103:8, 145:8; Joel 2:13). And as the experience of Jonah indicates, God's love was not limited to Israel. Jonah confessed God's concern for ungodly Nineveh: "I knew that you are a gracious and compassionate God, slow to anger and abounding in love, a God who relents from sending calamity" (Jon. 4:2). The good news of God's eternal love pervades the Old Testament from Genesis to Malachi.

God's love comes to fruition in the New Testament, as seen in the centerpiece of the Bible's message of love, John 3:16: "God so loved the world that he gave his one and only Son, that whoever believes in him shall not perish but have eternal life." John expanded on this central theme in his first letter: "This is how God showed his love among us: He sent his one and only Son into the world that we might live through him" (1 John 4:9). Jesus said, "Greater love has no one than this, that he lay down his life for his friends" (John 15:13). The apostle John echoed the thought, adding the importance of Christ's example for us: "This is how we know what love is: Jesus Christ laid down his life for us. And we ought to lay down our lives for our brothers" (1 John 3:16).

Paul marveled that God acted in love long before we knew we needed His love: "But God demonstrates his own love for us in this: While we were still sinners, Christ died for us" (Rom. 5:8). The sacrifice of the holy Son of God to redeem the sinful human race is the quintessence of love. No wonder John exults, "How great is the love the Father has lavished on us, that we should be called children of God! And that is what we are!" (1 John 3:1).

The Scriptures further assure us that God is tenacious, not tenuous, in His love for us. Romans 8:35, 38, 39 provides a stirring and encouraging view of God's commitment of love to us: "Who shall separate us from the love of Christ? Shall trouble or hardship or persecution or famine or nakedness or danger or sword? . . . I am convinced that neither death nor life, neither angels nor demons, neither the present nor the future, nor any powers, neither height nor depth, nor anything else in all creation, will be able to separate us from the love of God that is in Christ Jesus our Lord."

The love of God echoes throughout the New Testament. We see God the Father's love for His Son (Matt. 3:17; Mark 9:7) and the Son's love for His Father (John 14:31). Jesus tells us that His love for us is modeled after the Father's love for Him (John 15:9). We are commanded to respond to God's love for us by loving God (Matt. 22:37) and by loving others (John 13:34, 35; Rom. 13:8; 1 Pet. 1:22; 1 John 4:7), including our enemies (Matt. 5:44). But even when we love, our capacity to do so originates in God and His loving nature: "This is love: not that we loved God, but that he loved us and sent his Son as an atoning sacrifice for our sins" (1 John 4:10).

GOD OF LOVE AND GOD OF WRATH

"Wait a minute," many will interject. "If God is a God of love, why did He create hell, and why does He send people there?" Good question, and an important question. The Bible says that Jesus, who loved the world enough to die for it, will one day "punish those who do not know God and do not obey the gospel of our Lord Jesus. They will be punished with everlasting destruction and shut out from the presence of the Lord" (2 Thess. 1:8, 9). To unbelievers, Jesus will say, "Depart from me, you who are cursed, into the eternal fire prepared for the devil and his angels" (Matt. 25:41). In his vision, John noted that "if anyone's name was not found written in the book of life, he was thrown into the lake of fire" (Rev. 20:15). This place is described as one of torment from which there is no return (Luke 16:23–26), a place "where there will be weeping and gnashing of teeth" (Matt. 8:12). Isn't the existence of such a place incompatible with a God who is loving by nature?

The answer is no. Absolute love, far from being incompatible with hell, actually demands its existence. No one can force love from someone else. You choose to love God; He won't force you to love Him. God will, of course, do everything within His loving power to invite you to love Him. That's what the plan of redemption is all about. But for those who ultimately and finally refuse, God will not violate their freedom of destiny. As C. S. Lewis noted, there are only two kinds of people in the universe: those who say to God, "Your will be done," and those to whom God will say, "Your will be done." Jesus lamented compassionately His desire to gather His people like a hen gathers her chicks, "but you were not willing" (Matt. 23:37). Hell is the place provided by a long-suffering God for those who refuse to go His way. Having tried to win them, God will ultimately say to some, "All right, have it your way."

Cruel? Unloving? Not at all. Think about it: If God allowed unbelievers to enter heaven, it would be worse than hell for them. How could people who detest prayer and praise to God stand to be sentenced to a place where this activity goes on forever? If they felt uncomfortable for only an hour in church doing this, think of their discomfort if they had to do it forever! And since heaven is a place where people will bow in worship to God, how could a loving God force people to go there when they don't want to worship Him but rather hate Him or ignore Him as they have in this life? It is more congruent with the nature of divine love not to compel people to love Him against their will. Therefore God is actually merciful to unbelievers to provide for them a place consistent with their rejection of Him.

This doesn't mean that anyone who ends up in hell will actually enjoy being there. On the contrary, the Bible's description leaves no doubt about the undesirability of this eternal destination. People do not want to go to hell, but by refusing Christ they will go there. That's why we must continue to urge unbelieving family members, friends, neighbors, fellow students, and coworkers to yield to God's love and submit to His way. That is why we warn loved ones and strangers alike of the consequences of choosing to reject God and go their own way. We firmly believe that those whose backs are turned to God in anger or apathy can learn to love Him as we do. And yet, God will not force into heaven those who don't want to be there with Him. However undesirable their choice may be, they have made it, and they will have to live with it forever.

Someone may wonder, "What if someone in hell changes his

mind? Won't a loving God release a penitent person from hell and transfer him into heaven—better late than never?" The answer is no. People are in hell only because God knows they will never change their minds about Him. If a thousand more chances in life would have moved them to choose His way, God in love would have given those opportunities. But because He knows all things in advance, including the fact that some people will never change their minds, God lets them go and says, "Man is destined to die once, and after that to face judgment" (Heb. 9:27). God did not fail to display His love to them. But, sadly, even God's love failed to win them. He offered the opportunity for the best while allowing each person to choose less than His best. God the great lover amazingly permits the ultimate insult to His love: the rejection of it.

This description of God's love helps us better understand God's wrath. Wrath is the result of rejected love. As C. S. Lewis aptly observed, the only place in the universe where people will be free from the perturbations of love is hell. Hell is where love no longer works or woos, for it is no longer possible to win anyone there. It's not that God no longer loves. His radiant love still shines, but the effect is vastly different when love is rejected. The same sun that melts wax also hardens clay. The difference is not the source of the heat but the response of the object heated.

So it is with God's love. Where someone is not willing to respond to God's love, there is wrath. If you have ever tried to love someone who doesn't want to be loved, you have a small idea of the frustration of God's love. And if you have stubbornly or pridefully rejected the love others have extended, you have experienced a little bit of what hell is like. It is miserable to need love and want love and yet not open yourself to someone who loves you. Unbelievers are like buckets turned upside down under Niagara Falls. "Where is the love of God and the God of love?" they cry. "My life is empty and meaningless." Yet they refuse to turn their lives upward and let the waterfall of God's infinite love fill their lives. God is loving; His love flows like a mighty, ceaseless torrent. He wills the good of every individual, but His love cannot help them if they do not will their own greatest good by accepting His love.

There are many ways to deepen our knowledge and experience of the love of God and the God of love. Since God's creation is such an ever-present expression of His love, we ought to study and relish what God has made. King David wrote, "When I consider your heavens, the work of your fingers, the moon and the stars, which you have set in place, what is man that you are mindful of him, the son of man that you care for him?" (Ps. 8:3, 4). Society urges us to "stop and smell the roses." Scripture invites us to "consider" what God has made, look for His loving imprint on everything around us, and praise Him for his loving care.

Since human relationships reflect the nature of the God of love, we must encourage and affirm selfless human love wherever we find it. One bumper sticker suggests, "Practice random acts of kindness." The Bible says it this way: "As we have opportunity, let us do good to all people" (Gal. 6:10). People who love and serve others selflessly in Christ's name should be our heroes. Get close to these people, learn from them, and emulate their loving spirit.

Most of all, since the love of God and the God of love are most clearly presented in His Word, we must know the Scriptures. Study God's loving acts in Bible history from creation to redemption. Acquaint yourself with God's loving ways as stated in His commandments, Jesus' teachings, and the apostles' writings. Saturate yourself with the hymns and poems of the Psalms, many of which are love songs to God. The better you know God's Word, the better you know God. And the better you know God, the more clearly you will hear His heartbeat of love.

TOUGH QUESTIONS AND STRAIGHT ANSWERS ABOUT GOD'S LOVE

If nature is an expression of God's love, why does He allow natural evils, such as earthquakes, hurricanes, floods, and disease, that kill hundreds of people every year?

Natural disasters are the result of our sin, not an evidence that God's love is incomplete or ineffective. A transformation occurred on the earth after Adam and Eve disobeyed God in the garden. God said, "Cursed is the ground because of you; through painful toil you will eat of it all the days of your life. It will produce thorns and thistles for you. . . . By the sweat of your brow you will eat your food" (Gen. 3:17, 18). The world is tainted by physical evil, and it often brings "painful toil" into the lives of its inhabitants, even to those who love God. People who build homes and cities near a geological fault zone risk injury and death from earthquakes. If you live in a hurricane- or typhoon-prone region or flood plain, your crops and property may be swept away. If you fail to protect yourself from disease, you may become its victim.

It is important to understand that people who experience tragedy through natural disaster do not suffer because they are more wicked than those who are not affected (see Luke

13:3–5). Rather, physical evil comes into our lives for a number of different reasons. God is loving, and the only way we can love Him is freely. And free choice is the origin of evil.

1. *Some physical evils result from our free choices.* If you build a house near the San Andreas fault in California, you may be killed in an earthquake. If you buy a farm on the banks of the Mississippi River, you and your property may someday be swept away by a flood. If you overeat and under exercise, you run the risk of a heart attack.

2. *Some physical evils result from choosing to do nothing.* Laziness may lead to poverty. Putting off a routine physical examination may allow an undetected cancer to become untreatable. Unwillingness to break the bad habit of driving while tired may cause a fatal crash.

3. *Some physical evils result from the free choices of others.* Child abuse, drive-by shootings, muggings, and alcohol-related traffic deaths are examples of how innocent people suffer evil at the hands of irresponsible or evil people.

4. *Some physical evil is a by-product of good activities.* A few people who go to the lake to sail or swim will drown there. Skiers, mountain-climbers, and skydivers are sometimes injured or killed in their sport. Even a car trip to church can end in severe injury or death.

5. *Some physical evils result from the activity of evil spirits.* Job's sufferings were attributed to Satan (Job 1:6–12). Evil spirits oppress and afflict people with diseases (Matt. 17:14–18; Luke 13:11).

6. *Some physical evils are God-given warnings of greater physical evils.* A toothache can help prevent future tooth

decay. Chest pains, if heeded, may prevent needless death. The grief of losing a parent to cancer may prompt family members to submit to cancer screenings.

7. *Some physical evils are God-given warnings about moral evils.* Pain and tragedy get our attention and cause us to seek God as do few other experiences. Paul spoke about the wrath of God leading to repentance (Rom. 2:4). C. S. Lewis spoke of pain as God's megaphone.

8. *Some physical evils are permitted to prompt moral development.* Without tribulation there would be no patience. Joseph's brothers sold him into slavery, but he forgave them and said, "You intended to harm me, but God intended it for good" (Gen. 50:20). Job suffered much and said, "When [God] has tested me, I will come forth as gold" (Job 23:10).

9. *Some physical evils occur because higher forms of life live on lower ones.* In this physical world, birds eat worms, cats eat birds, and thoughtless children torture cats. Similarly, people and forces greater than us plague us or hurt us without just cause. Sometimes we can defend ourselves against them, and sometimes, despite our best efforts, we cannot.

So why doesn't our omnipotent God miraculously intervene and prevent physical evil from happening? First, God does sometimes intervene (when He deems it necessary to His overall redemptive plan), but to do so regularly, He would have to interfere with the full exercise of free choice, leaving us with a world something less than fully moral. Second, in a world of constant divine intervention against evil actions, all moral learning would cease. We would never experience bad consequences from wrong choices and thus realize our potential for moral progress or achievement.

Why does a loving God allow His human creations to mistreat each other? Why does He allow people to become murderers, rapists, child abusers, abortionists, and so on?

The real question behind these concerns is, "Why did God make creatures with free choice when He knew some would choose evil?" Because creating people with free will was the best possible choice of at least four alternatives open to a loving God. First, He could have avoided sin completely by choosing not to create a world at all. But God is love, and like a loving father, He wanted a family with whom to share His love. Second, He could not have chosen to make a world populated by creatures who love Him without choice. Forced love is a contradiction in terms. Robots don't really love; they are programmed to respond. Third, hypothetically He could have created a world where people were free to choose but would never sin. However, since people are free to choose to sin, this never happened. Fourth, He could have created a world where people are free and choose to sin—which is what He did. So God created Adam and Eve with the capacity to obey and disobey, to love and not to love Him and others. They ultimately chose to disobey, and as a consequence sin entered our race.

To some it may seem a blatant contradiction to God's holiness that He would select the only option in which evil could occur. Free human beings can—and do—opt to reject Him, mock Him, and disobey Him to His face. And human beings all too readily violate and hurt each other. Yet sin was the possibility God allowed in order to love us and to allow us to love Him in the best possible way.

LOVE IN
EVERYDAY LANGUAGE

5

L ove—the word slips into our conversations almost unnoticed every day.

- Don't you just love it?

- Sure, I'd love to do lunch next week.

- I heard a great story; you'll love it.

- Wow, I love the acceleration and handling of this car!

- My kitten is so cute. I just love him.

- I wouldn't take that job for love or money.

- I love these crisp autumn mornings.

- I love you, honey, with all my heart.

- You gotta love our team!

Turn on the radio or TV any time of the day or night. You can't get away from love. It is crooned on music stations, dramatized (often *melo*dramatized!) in soap operas, humorized in sitcoms, and mocked in trash-talk shows.

- Love can't be wrong if it feels so right.

- I'm having our love child.

- If you can't be with the one you love, love the one you're with.

- I love what you do for me.

- If you really love me, show me.

- What the world needs now is love, sweet love.

- I want your love, I need your love (O baby, baby, baby).

The word *love* has a broad spectrum of meanings in our culture. So when we talk about love these days, it's important to know exactly what kind of love we're talking about. For example, if a man doesn't see the difference between loving old Bubba, his hunting dog, loving his favorite putter, and loving his wife, he's in deep trouble—with his wife, not the dog. A woman must be aware that her love for her job, her love for the dahlias in her garden, and her love for her children are different levels of love. And if we are going to grasp the vital importance of love as the ultimate right thing to do—the love that flows from the very nature of God, we had better know if we're talking about the kind of love that saturates our culture today from such potent centers of influence as Hollywood, Nashville, Madison Avenue, and MTV.

LOVE IS . . .

The apostle Paul dedicates an entire chapter to the topic of love (1 Cor. 13). In one section, he dashes off a flurry of descriptive words and phrases: "Love is patient, love is kind. It does not envy, it does not boast, it is not proud. It is not rude, it is not self-seeking, it is not easily angered, it keeps no record of wrongs. Love does not delight in evil but rejoices with the truth. It always protects, always trusts, always hopes, always perseveres" (vv. 4–7). When you ask Christians to define real love—the kind of love that is God's nature and that we should exercise—they will often point to this paragraph or parrot some of these phrases.

First Corinthians 13 is a good description of what love *does* and *does not* do. And from this description and others in Scripture, we can derive a concise statement defining what love *is. Love wills and works for the good of the one loved.* Stated another way, *love is making the health, happiness, and growth of another person as important to you as your own.* Is our health, happiness, and growth important to us? Of course! We all work hard at staying happy, safe, secure, and prosperous. Anyone with only a few grams of ambition wants to grow as a Christian, move up the ladder in his or her job, find and deepen friendships, and generally improve his or her lot in life. It's part of our makeup as humans to not only survive but also flourish as individuals in every way possible.

True love demands that we care as much for the success and development of others as we do for ourselves. This was Paul's instruction in Philippians 2:4: "Each of you should look not only to your own interests, but also to the interests of others." Paul also wrote, "Love does no harm to its neighbor" (Rom. 13:10). Instead of doing harm, love does what is good and right to others. Remember: We all have a sense of what is good and right, a sense of morality. We discover this personal belief about right and wrong when we determine how we expect to be treated by other people. Love simply says, "Treat others right, the way you want to be treated." It all goes back to the Golden Rule given to us by Jesus: "In everything, do to others what you would have them do to you" (Matt. 7:12).

How does this definition play out in everyday life? Here are a few examples. If you think it's reasonable for your wife to keep the kids occupied while you watch Monday night football, love requires that you give her a "Mom's night out" when she requests or needs one. If you expect your boss to treat you with respect, love requires that you treat him or her with respect and not speak ill of your boss to coworkers or customers. If you think your pastor ought to be more attentive to your spiritual needs, love requires that you do your part to meet his or her needs, such as praying for him consistently or defending him or her against gossip.

The loving thing to do in most situations is not difficult to discern. Simply put yourself in the shoes of people involved and ask, "What is the best I could wish for if it were me?" When you determine the answer, love requires that you do the best that you have the opportunity and ability to do.

When we make the health, happiness, and growth of others a prime priority, we are following the example of the God of love. God wills only the best for every person, as seen in His deeds.

First, He created us in His image and likeness (Gen. 1:27). He could have made us in the image of angels or other beautiful creatures. But humankind was the crown of God's creation, and His best for us was that we reflect His nature. So God made humans "a little lower than the heavenly beings and crowned [them] with glory and honor" (Ps. 8:5). What better model could we ask for than to be formed in God's image and crowned with His glory and honor?

Second, God wills our best by sustaining our life on this planet through His loving power. Ezra prayed, "You alone are the Lord. You made the heavens, . . . the earth and all that is on it, the seas and all that is in them. You give life to everything" (Neh. 9:6). Paul wrote, "All things were created by him and for him. He is before all things, and in him all things hold together" (Col. 1:16, 17). God not only gave us life, He also sustains our life.

Hebrews 1:3 states that Christ sustains "all things by his powerful word." If He ceased to sustain us for an instant, planet Earth, everything on it—including us—and the universe around it would disappear. We owe our existence to the God who sustains us as an ongoing expression of His love.

Third, God demonstrated that He wills the best for sinful humanity by redeeming us at great cost. When Jesus Christ died on the cross, He did so for all people (2 Cor. 5:15), even those who never respond to His love. John declared, "He is the atoning sacrifice for our sins, and not only for ours but also for the sins of the whole world" (1 John 2:2). Furthermore, God desires that no one perish but that everyone comes to repentance (2 Pet. 3:9). The best-case scenario for God's human creation is that we live in fellowship with Him through time and eternity. In His love, God has acted to make that scenario a reality for all who go His way.

The fact that some people refuse the gift of salvation, choosing instead to go their own ways, demonstrates a vital characteristic of true love. The love that comes from God's nature, the love we are commanded to express in all our relationships, He gives with no demand for return. "God so loved the world that he gave his one and only Son, that whoever believes . . ." (John 3:16). The operative word here is *whoever.* When God gave His Son, He was fully aware that some would believe and others would not. John wrote, "He came to that which was his own, but his own did not receive him" (John 1:11).

In reality, even our freedom to choose is a love gift from God, who considers it in our best interest not to force us to return His love. God *desires* all people to love Him, but He does not *demand* that we do. Similarly, love for others is *commanded* but not *demanded* by God. And yet Christ died for all, even those who turn their backs on Him. Consider Jesus' examples of love. He knew that Judas would betray Him, but He loved him and called him to be a disciple anyway. When the crowd cried, "Crucify Him!" Jesus responded, "Father, forgive them, for they do not know what they are doing" (Luke 23:34). God's love persists whether we receive it or not. Paul wrote, "If we are faithless, he will remain faithful, for he cannot disown himself" (2 Tim. 2:13). To give with no demand for return is in God's nature, and therefore it is the nature of true love, for God is love.

Like Christ, you may also face rejection when you decide to love as God loves. You may "do to others what you would have them do to you" only to have your loving deed ignored or thrown back in your face. For example, when your neighbor goes out of town, you volunteer to feed and exercise his dog. In your mind, it's the neighborly thing to do. But when you ask your neighbor to reciprocate, he replies, "Are you kidding? I don't have time, and your dog is a big, slobbering nuisance." Or you buy your child a surprise gift, and she complains, "What a dumb present. It's ugly, and I don't want it." Or you stay late to help a coworker finish up, only to hear, "I don't need your help. Besides, you're just trying to kiss up to the boss."

Left to the guidance of our emotions in situations like these, we may be tempted to forget about future opportunities to love these people. But genuine love doesn't give with a return in mind. Love gives because it cares about the health, happiness, and growth of others—period. Whether its actions or tokens are received, love continues to give. Whenever you withhold your love because someone ignores it or doesn't appreciate it the way he or she should, you're not loving with the love that comes from God.

Similarly, love gives even when we don't like everything about those we choose to love. This too is a reflection of God's love. God hates sin to the point that He can't even look on it (Hab. 1:13). In our sinful condition, there was nothing about us for God to like. Yet He loved us and gave His very best for us, His only Son. Following His example, you may decide to go caroling in a nursing home at Christmas even though you don't like smelling the smells or seeing the sad faces and emaciated bodies of the residents. You may volunteer to care for your unfriendly neighbor's dog again even though you don't like the way he talks about your Fifi. You may continue to offer help to a suspicious, ungrateful coworker. Or you may determine to pray for government leaders whose policies and positions clash with your own. Whenever you give yourself lovingly to serve someone, even if that person is offensive to you in some way, you are demonstrating God's love.

A PROVIDER AND PROTECTOR

God has given us another helpful perspective of the kind of love that is His nature and should be our practice. The picture is found in Paul's instructions in Ephesians 5:28, 29: "In this same way, husbands ought to love their wives as their own bodies. He who loves his wife loves himself. After all, no one ever hated his own body, but he feeds and cares for it, just as Christ does the church." There is more to this instruction than a specific application to husbands about loving their wives. Notice several things from these lines.

First, the kind of love Paul talks about for husbands is the kind of love Christ exercises for the church. When God asks us to love, He always bids us to follow His example. He doesn't call us to do something for which He isn't already the perfect example. True love always has God as its source.

Second, the instruction to husbands here reflects Jesus' commandment about loving others in Matthew 22:39: "Love your neighbor as yourself." In other words, not only husbands but all Christians are to love others as we love ourselves. The Golden Rule again comes into focus: We are to love others as we desire and expect them to love us. This command to husbands is an application of the commandment to love others.

Third, these verses tell us exactly how we are to love ourselves and, subsequently, how we are to love others: "No one ever hated his own body, but he feeds and cares for it" (Eph. 5:29). *Feed and care for* are key terms in understanding how we are to make the health, happiness, and growth of others as important to us as our own. Just as we are all concerned and active to make sure our physical, emotional, and spiritual needs are met, so we are to be concerned and active to meet the needs of others, not just our spouses as Paul instructs, but everyone, as Jesus commands elsewhere. That's love.

The King James Version uses two beautifully descriptive words in this verse: *nourish* and *cherish*. Just as we are careful to nourish and cherish our own bodies, we are to nourish and cherish others in love.

To nourish means to bring to maturity. It pictures the growth of young Jesus in Nazareth as described in Luke 2:52:

"Jesus grew in wisdom and stature, and in favor with God and men." To nourish means to care for and contribute to the whole person: mentally, physically, spiritually, and socially. Love is a provider. It requires that we provide for the health, happiness, and growth of others in order to bring them to maturity, just as we provide for our own health, happiness, and growth.

To cherish means to protect from the elements. Imagine a nest of newborn eaglets high on a mountain crag, exposed to the sky. An angry thunderstorm is rolling in. The mother eagle swoops down to the nest and spreads her wings over the eaglets to protect them from the pounding rain and swirling wind. That's a picture of what it means to cherish.

Ephesians 5:29 tells us that it is natural for us to cherish ourselves, that is, to protect ourselves from anything that may endanger our mental, physical, spiritual, and social well-being. We buckle up and drive safely to prevent physical injury or death on the highway. We monitor our fat and calorie intake to keep our bodies healthy. We learn to turn away when tempted to compromise our obedience to Christ. We stay away from people who are a bad influence on our beliefs or behavior. In short, we generally guard ourselves against anything that negatively affects our lives. Love is a protector as well as a provider. Love requires that we do what we can to protect others from anything that may detour or hinder their maturity, just as we protect ourselves.

Love means to nourish and cherish, that is, to provide and protect. How does this play out practically? For husbands and wives, it means allowing each other occasional breaks from the children for such activities as personal devotions, classes and seminars, or hobbies like fishing, shopping, working in the shop, or scouring garage sales. For dating couples, it means that you will provide a wholesome environment for your relationship to grow and protect each other from situations of moral compromise. For parents, it means that you will take care that your children eat healthy meals and live in safety. And it means that you will provide wholesome at-home entertainment and education opportunities for your children and protect them from harmful videos, TV programs, and music. It means that you may provide good reading materials to that Christian friend who is addicted to trashy novels that are polluting his mind.

In his message to husbands, Paul provides another beautiful picture of our goal as we provide for and protect our family members, friends, neighbors, coworkers, and others. Christ's goal for the church He loves is "to make her holy, cleansing her by the washing with water through the word, and to present her to himself as a radiant church, without stain or wrinkle or any other blemish, but holy and blameless" (Eph. 5:26–27). His goal is to provide for our maturity and protect us from anything that can stain and scar our lives. It is divine work that flows from divine love.

Since we are to love others as Christ loves us, our goal is to treat people so that we contribute to their holiness and radiance as God's children and protect them from the stain of sin and hurt. Ask yourself about relationships and personal encounters:

- Did I add to her beauty and brightness as a person or detract from it?

- Did I encourage him toward maturity in some way or discourage him?

- Did I urge him toward holiness, or did I tempt him toward sin?

- Is she more pure as a result of our interaction or more stained?

Love always seeks to leave people more healthy and more mature than we found them, because that is Christ's ongoing, loving work in our lives.

TOUGH QUESTIONS AND STRAIGHT ANSWERS ABOUT TRUE LOVE

How do you know if you truly love someone?

Contrary to popular opinion, love is more than a good feeling. The key to true love is to obey God by loving others beyond mere feelings of devotion. Whether with a romantic partner, a family member, a coworker, a neighbor, or a stranger, ask yourself: Is the health, happiness, and growth of this person as important to me as my own? Am I involved in bringing this person to maturity at every level: mentally, physically, spiritually, and socially? Am I ready to protect this person from any elements that will threaten his or her well-being or deter his or her growth? Am I encouraging this person toward holiness and godliness instead of compromise and sin? If you can answer these questions in the affirmative, you truly love that person.

How do you love someone when you don't feel like loving him or her?

Love isn't something you necessarily feel; it's something you do. Good feelings may accompany loving deeds, but we are commanded to love whether we feel like it or not. Jesus didn't feel like giving His life to redeem humankind (Matt. 26:38–39). On the night before His crucifixion, Jesus was in agony in the garden. He asked the Father if there was any way He could avoid the cross. But He loved the Father and yielded to His will, and He loved us and became the sacrifice for our sin. That's how we are to love. We act on the basis of our obedience and love for God, who commands us to love others as He has loved us.

The bonus for us when we begin to love people we don't feel like loving is that eventually we can learn to like them too. When we do the right thing in love, even though we don't feel like doing it, we can learn to like doing it. Good feelings often follow right, loving choices and actions.

When we love others, we are to seek what is best for them. But how can we know what is best for someone else?

You can't know what is best for every person in every situation. But there are some guidelines that can help you discern the best for people in most situations. First, put yourself in their shoes. What is the best possible good you would hope for in the situation? Once you answer that question, do to others as you would have them do to you. Second, consider the Scriptures. The more you know God's Word, the better prepared you are to guide people into healthy, productive behavior. Third, recall your experience as a Christian. Lessons you have learned the hard way may help guide others to the best while avoiding unnecessary disappointment and pain. Fourth, seek the counsel of mature Christians. Proverbs 15:22 says, "Plans fail for lack of counsel, but with many advisers they succeed." Fifth, trust the guidance of the Holy Spirit. In every situation, ask God to show His best for the person's life.

Be aware, however, that even when you have the best for others at heart, you cannot force your guidance upon them. Everyone is responsible for his or her own life. You may want to express your love to a friend, for example, by protecting her from the consequences of drug addiction. You know getting straight is in her best interest. You can counsel her, pray with her, even arrange an intervention for her if you feel it is necessary. But she has to choose the best *for herself;* you can't choose it for her. And if your efforts fail and your friend makes the wrong choice, you are not to blame. If people reject your love, it doesn't mean that you have failed to love. You can only offer to provide and protect; people must choose to accept your offer.

J eff, a college sophomore, attends the frosh mixer to meet girls. He is not disappointed. This year's freshman class seems to be well stocked with good-looking, available females. Then, on his way to the punch bowl, it happens. He sees Meg for the first time, and his mouth drops open in amazement. Meg isn't just good looking, she's a goddess. Jeff is stunned by her silky hair, sparkling eyes, cover-girl complexion, and fashion-model figure. He has never seen anyone so beautiful.

Jeff's heart begins to race, his mouth goes dry, and his palms begin to sweat. All he wants to do is get close to Meg, meet her, talk to her, touch her. Finally, he finds the courage to introduce himself. They talk for a few minutes, then Meg excuses herself with a flirty smile that turns Jeff's knees to Jell-O.

For the next two weeks, Jeff can't eat, sleep, or study. Meg's face is in his mind constantly. He plans his day around bumping into her "accidentally" on campus. They talk again briefly—in the library, in the Student Union. They meet for lunch a couple of times, he calls her in the dorm. Jeff can't get enough of Meg, and she seems interested in him. On their first official date, they hold hands in the movie, and Jeff's heart races. After getting to know Meg better, he is even more impressed. Finally, one moonlit night, Jeff ecstatically blurts out, "Meg, you're so wonderful. I just want to be with you."

Meg sighs, "I want to be with you, too, Jeff." It's obvious that Jeff and Meg are falling in love. But what kind of love are they experiencing?

Not all expressions of human love are as altruistic as the love that protects and provides with no demand for return. There are at least two other types of love in human relationships. One is a *self-centered* love that focuses more on pleasure gained than given in a relationship. The other is a *mutual* love in which persons are involved in a give-and-take relationship. These are contrasted with what we are calling true love, an *unselfish* love that gives without demand for anything in return; seeks the health, happiness, and growth of others; and commits to provide and protect. Sometimes the three loves are identified by their Greek names: *eros*, *philia*, and *agape*. In his excellent book, *The Four Loves*, C. S. Lewis calls them *eros*, *friendship*, and *charity*, respectively, while adding a fourth, affection, to represent the Greek *storge*, or love for family. We will look at the first three.

EROS: YOU MAKE ME FEEL SO GOOD

Although other types of love may come into play later in their relationship, Jeff and Meg have been drawn together by eros.

Jeff pursued Meg because her appearance pleased his senses and aroused his masculine appetites. He stayed in pursuit because, like taking a drug, being with Meg brought him pleasure, satisfaction, even a sense of euphoria. In short, Jeff wanted to be with Meg because she made him feel good. The fact that she wanted him too only intensified the pleasure.

That's eros, love that craves self-satisfaction. At its very worst, eros is animalistic lust. C. S. Lewis describes it as a man seeking pleasure for which a woman happens to be the necessary piece of apparatus. How much he really cares about the woman can be discovered five minutes after he gets what he wants.

At best, eros is the deep physical and emotional longing for someone of the opposite sex, as modeled by Jeff and Meg. C. S. Lewis calls it falling or being in love, and it can happen quite apart from insistent or premature sexual desire. Lewis differentiates between noble and ignoble eros: "Sexual desire, without eros wants [sensory pleasure] in itself; eros wants the beloved. . . . Eros makes a man really want, not a woman, but one particular woman. In some mysterious but quite indisputable fashion the lover desires the beloved herself, not the pleasure she can give."[1]

There's nothing wrong with "being in love" in the best sense, as those who have fallen in love will attest. But eros is a poor foundation for a lasting, healthy relationship. In reality, eros is not even necessary for a successful marriage. Consider the number of cultures where marriages are contracted by the parents before the bride and groom even meet, let alone fall in love. Having been joined together as husband and wife with little or nothing to say about it, these couples set about the task of establishing a relationship based on something other than magnetic attraction. And where a couple wills and works for the best in each other, the marriage succeeds. If the love between a man and woman is going to flourish, it must expand from self-satisfying, romantic eros to an other-centered, other-satisfying love.

PHILIA: YOU'VE GOT A FRIEND

Walter and Ezra have been meeting on Saturday afternoons to play chess for years. Along the way they met Rube and Chester, who share their intense love for the game. Every Saturday at noon, rain or shine, the four men meet in Lapner's Park, spread out two well-worn chessboards, and play several games. None of them has ever said so, but each would agree that Saturday afternoon around the chessboard is the highlight of the week. Sometimes a stranger will come along and challenge one of them to a game, and the challenge is always accepted. But the newcomers rarely last a month, while Walter, Ezra, Rube, and Chester are as much of a fixture in the park on Saturdays as the tarnished statue of Harvey Lapner, the town's founder.

The four friends talk during their games, but the subject matter is generally limited. They mostly chat about their most common interest: chess-openings, gambits, great matches they remember, the strategies of the masters. Walter and his wife had Ezra and Maggie over to dinner several years earlier before Maggie succumbed to cancer. But they didn't have much to talk about besides chess. Since then the two men have seen each other only at the park. They have never met Rube's wife or been to his home. And none of the three even knows where Chester, who is a bachelor, lives.

Occasionally the four chess friends will discuss their careers (two of them are retired, the others are semiretired), brag about their children and grandchildren, or argue politics. But it all gets back to chess eventually. If they didn't have chess in common, they probably wouldn't have met in the first place, or having met, they wouldn't have become friends. After all these years, Walter, Ezra, Rube, and Chester might admit that they would do anything for each other. But they offer little and demand even less of each other. They just play chess.

Friendship love, or philia, is a relationship of mutual admiration and give and take based on a common interest. Lewis writes, "Friendship must be about something, even if it were only an enthusiasm for dominoes or white mice. Those who have nothing can share nothing; those who are going nowhere can have no fellow travelers."[2] Philia is generally less self-centered than eros. But if one member takes too much and gives too little, the friendship may be on shaky ground. Friendship is also less emotionally intense than eros. In contrasting the two, Lewis says, "Lovers are always talking to one another about their love; friends hardly ever about their friendship. Lovers are normally face to face, absorbed in each other; friends, side by side, absorbed in some common interest. Above all, eros (while it lasts) is necessarily between two only. But two, far from being the necessary number for friendship, is not even the best."[3]

Friends take care of each other when needs arise, but that's not principally why friends are friends. They come together over a common task, idea, activity, cause, belief, or experience. Meeting special needs or responding to emergencies for each other are seen almost as interruptions to the real purpose of the friendship. As Walter said to Ezra after Maggie's funeral, "So, are you planning to be at the park next Saturday?"

If the common interest between friends ceases to exist, a higher level of love must become active to keep friends together. For example, when Walter suffered a debilitating stroke, Rube and Chester felt sorry for him, but they never went to see him. They were more concerned about finding a fourth for their weekly chess tournaments in the park. Ezra, however, called on Walter in the hospital. When Walter went home, Ezra came to visit two or three times a week. Walter could no longer play chess with his friend. In fact, he couldn't even talk about chess, having completely lost his ability to speak. Yet his wife told Ezra that Walter always seemed more alert when his old friend sat beside the wheelchair and rambled on about chess and politics. Ezra received virtually nothing from Walter in return, yet he continued to come. Ezra's love for his friend had reached a new level: a sacrificial love that demands nothing in return.

AGAPE: LOVE WITHOUT STRINGS

Agape is love that is *of* God and *from* God. It is the love that gives without demand for return. It is the love that makes the health, happiness, and growth of others as important to us as our own. It is the love that is committed to provide and protect, to contribute to an individual's purity. Added to eros, agape can transform a romance into a dynamic, fulfilling marriage. Added to philia, agape can transform a common friendship into a warm and meaningful bond of unselfish service.

C. S. Lewis calls agape "gift-love." Agape is the love of God who, needing nothing, "loves into existence wholly superfluous creatures in order that He may love and perfect them."[4] God's gift-love was supremely demonstrated in the gift of His Son for our redemption. John wrote, "This is love: not that we loved God, but that he loved us and sent his Son as an atoning sacrifice for our sins" (1 John 4:10).

Gift-love is available to God's human creation to exercise in at least two ways. The first is in our best attempt to love unselfishly and sacrificially. Lewis calls it *human* gift-love. There is a limited measure of agape built into our nature. You can find many Christians as well as avowed non-Christians sacrificially giving of themselves and their means to help others. Yet human gift-love, though clearly generous and other-centered, is always qualified. Left to ourselves, we are incapable of loving as God loves. We love those we find in some way lovable. We love people who are grateful and deserving or whose needs most touch our sympathies. In human agape we may love in the best ways humanly possible, much more nobly than the self-centeredness of eros or the give and take of philia. Ezra's loving visits to Walter after the stroke certainly demonstrated a higher love than the dedicated friendship around the chess board. But the most sacrificial love humanly possible still falls short of God's expression of agape.

The better exercise of agape is what Lewis calls *divine* gift-love, which is the love of God—in reality, the indwelling God of love—working in us and through us to protect and provide for others. Only God's love can allow us to love anyone and everyone without strings, or as Lewis says, "to love what is not naturally lovable; lepers, criminals, enemies, morons, the sulky, the superior and the sneering."[5] It is to this level of love that Christ called us when He said, "Love your enemies" (Matt. 5:44); "Love your neighbor as yourself" (Matt. 22:39); "Love each other as I have loved you" (John 15:12).

Paul was speaking of divine agape when he instructed, "Do everything in love" (1 Cor. 16:14); "Live a life of love, just as Christ loved us and gave himself up for us" (Eph. 5:2). Peter echoed the command: "Above all, love each other deeply" (1

Pet. 4:8). So did John: "Let us love one another, for love comes from God. . . . Since God so loved us, we also ought to love one another" (1 John 4:7, 11).

But if you think that the divine gift-love Christians are to exercise is a soft-soap, become-the-world's-doormat kind of love peddled in some circles today, consider the further implications of agape.

First, *love involves discipline.* God is the perfect loving Father, yet He "disciplines those he loves, and he punishes everyone he accepts as a son" (Heb. 12:6). Proverbs 13:24 declares, "He who spares the rod hates his son, but he who loves him is careful to discipline him." Love does not go soft on wrongdoers and let things slide. Love confronts those who are out of line—a disobedient child, a lazy employee, a church member involved in obvious sin, a dishonest boss—because confrontive love will ultimately protect them from the painful consequences of their misbehavior. Love accepts the offender while firmly rejecting the offense. For example, love for an addicted friend or relative may move you to commit that person to treatment against his or her wishes.

Second, *love can be tough.* Jesus, the personification of God's love, displayed anger at His opponents (Mark 3:5), verbally blasted hypocrites (Matt. 23), and physically expelled the greedy merchants from the temple (John 2). Love for your boss may require you to risk your job by confronting him or her over a shady deal. Love may direct you to debate an ungodly civic leader who is leading the community away from morality. Divine love is patient and kind, but it is anything but spineless and subservient. It can be tough when necessary in order to protect and provide.

Third, *love can fail.* The proper translation of 1 Corinthians 13:8 is not "Love never fails" but "Love never ends." The sad truth is that not everyone is won over by love. God loved Adam and Eve fully and perfectly in the Garden, but His love failed to prevent them from choosing to sin. God's love for the unbeliever never ends, but it does fail, as evidenced by the reality of hell and the untold numbers who have chosen to spend eternity there. Yet God's love is eternal because He is eternal. He continues to display His love to the world even though some will reject Him. We also must exercise divine agape with the realization that our efforts may fail to make a difference in the ones we love. In other words, you may commit your time, energy, and means to protect and provide for someone only to find that he or she isn't interested in you, your provision, or your protection. However, the old saying applies well to divine agape: It is better to have loved and lost than never to have loved at all. Even God loved and lost one-third of His angels (Rev. 12:4). Jesus loved and lost one of His apostles (John 17:12). And He loved the whole world (John 3:16) but many will be lost (Matt. 7:13, 14).

Furthermore, love is not an option for the Christian. Not only is love a universal moral absolute (all people expect to be loved and therefore ought to love others), it is also a biblical imperative on two vital levels, as we shall explore next.

TOUGH QUESTIONS AND STRAIGHT ANSWERS ABOUT TYPES OF LOVE

Is it wrong for Christians to "fall in love," or should all our dating and marriage relationships be based only on agape?

If all eros is evil, we would have to delete Solomon's Song of Songs from our Bibles. Physical attraction and sexual desire between a man and a woman are natural and normal, part of God's design. Solomon's poem extols the erotic delights in the marriage relationship. The love story of Jacob and Rachel also portrays eros in a positive light, even in a culture where marriages were generally arranged by parents: "Rachel was lovely in form, and beautiful. Jacob was in love with Rachel. . . . So Jacob served seven years to get Rachel, but they seemed like only a few days to him because of his love for her" (Gen. 29:17, 18, 20). Proverbs 5:18, 19 encourages, "May you rejoice in the wife of your youth. . . . May her breasts satisfy you always, may you ever be captivated by her love." Paul wrote, "The wife's body does not belong to her alone but also to her husband. In the same way, the husband's body does not belong to him alone but also to his wife" (1 Cor. 7:4). The writer of Hebrews declared, "Marriage should be honored by all, and the marriage bed kept pure" (13:4). It's apparent from Scripture that falling in love, being in love, and enjoying the erotic and sexual dimension of love within marriage are gifts from God.

As with all of God's gifts to us, the problem with eros among Christians is misuse. Physical attraction and sexual desire must be kept within the boundaries God has established. For example, an unmarried couple may be strongly drawn together by eros, but sexual activity for them must be reserved until marriage. For a married couple, eros provides spark, excitement, recreation, and diversion from life's trials and boredom. But attraction to or desire for someone other than one's spouse must be dismissed and not acted upon. Extramarital sexual activity is sin (1 Thess. 4:3–8).

Furthermore, physical attraction and sexual desire is an insufficient foundation for a lasting, healthy relationship between a man and a woman. Eros may serve well to bring two people together, but it was never designed to keep them together. Sexual attraction may diminish over time, and sexual function may cease due to illness or injury. A marriage dependent on erotic feelings and good sex is bound to fail. A relationship must grow to include friendship and unselfish agape if it is to succeed as a Christian marriage.

Where should Christians draw the line in our love relationships with non-Christians?

Regarding agape, the Scriptures give us plenty of territory in which to work. Paul instructed, "Let no debt remain outstanding, except the continuing debt to love one another, for he who loves his fellowman has fulfilled the law" (Rom. 13:8) and "As we have opportunity, let us do good to all people" (Gal. 6:10). Generally speaking, we are to consider the health, happiness, and growth of anyone and everyone we meet as important to us as our own. Practically speaking, there are not enough hours in the day for us to love everyone around us in need of health, happiness, and growth. That's why Paul says, "As we have opportunity." There are scriptural priorities to consider when it comes to providing for and protecting others. We will consider these priorities in following chapters.

Regarding philia or friendship, many Christians believe that we should not have good friends among unbelievers. They quote James 4:4: "Anyone who chooses to be a friend of the world becomes an enemy of God." But this verse is talking about being friends with the world's *system* of believing and behaving, not relating to the world's *people*. Jesus spent so much time among unbelievers that He was taunted as a friend of sinners (Luke 15:2). He attended their banquets and visited their homes (Luke 19:1–10). It was His openness to and pursuit of "sinners" like Zacchaeus that exemplified His mission "to seek and to save what was lost" (Luke 19:10).

Jesus' words introduce a key term regarding any friendships we may develop with unbelievers: *influence*. If you can be involved in such a friendship and still maintain a positive influence for Christ, the relationship may be all right. However, if you are being negatively influenced in the friendship and your Christian beliefs and witness are compromised, the friendship is probably unhealthy. In other words, if your bowling team members are influencing you toward worldliness more than you are influencing them toward Christ, you need to find another hobby. But if you sign up for the team in order to have fun and share Christ through your life and words and you are able to control the direction of influence, your friendship parallels Christ's friendship with the "sinners" of His day.

Regarding eros and unbelievers, the Scriptures are quite clear: "Do not be yoked together with unbelievers. For what do righteousness and wickedness have in common? Or what fellowship can light have with darkness?" (2 Cor. 6:14). For unmarried Christians, an eros attraction to unbelievers is a temptation that can lead to an unequal union. You may argue, "But if I go out with him, I can lead him to Christ. If I don't, he may never hear about Christ." Don't fool yourself. If you are emotionally involved, you will do better to pray for his salvation than to risk a close relationship of compromise.

For married Christians, a strong eros attraction to an unbelieving neighbor, coworker, or stranger should be regarded as a serious potential danger to the sanctity of your marriage. Stand against all tempting thoughts and feelings in Christ's power. Avoid socializing with that person or fantasizing about that person. If necessary, admit your attraction to your spouse, a friend, or a counselor who can pray with you and hold you accountable.

THE LOVE IMPERATIVE

7

Many years ago I (Josh) spent a summer teaching at Arrowhead Springs, Campus Crusade's former headquarters in the foothills of the San Bernardino Mountains in Southern California. During that summer, my family and I lived in Blue Jay, a quaint little town beside beautiful Lake Arrowhead in the mountains. So every day I drove down the mountain to the Springs twice: once in the morning and again after lunch.

It's hot in the San Bernardino Valley during the summer, with temperatures often breaking the 100-degree mark. During my trips up and down the mountain, I often saw cars on the shoulder of the steep, winding road to the summit with their hoods open, belching steam from their radiators. It was soon apparent to me that my ministry for God at the Springs was rather hollow if I didn't do something to help the poor stranded motorists. All my talk about loving God was meaningless if I didn't show love for these people in need.

So I came up with a plan. I bought four large water jugs, filled them, and stowed them in my trunk. Whenever I came upon an overheated car on my daily journeys on the mountain, I pulled over and offered to fill the radiator with water. People were overjoyed at the offer and very grateful for the help. Once the radiator was full, I offered a copy of my book, *More Than a Carpenter*, and talked to the motorists about Christ. It was one of the most rewarding summers of ministry I have ever experienced.

Love is an absolutely binding imperative for the Christian. God is love and those born of God must express His love. Jesus said, "By this all men will know that you are my disciples, if you love one another" (John 13:35). And love always goes in two directions at once. When you love people in Christ's name, you are also loving God. Jesus taught that when we minister to anyone in need of love and care, we are ministering to Him (Matt. 25:34–40). And when you love God, you will also love people. Like faith and action, the two are virtually inseparable. James declared, "Faith by itself, if it is not accompanied by action, is dead" (James 2:17). Similarly, John wrote, "If anyone says, 'I love God,' yet hates his brother, he is a liar. For anyone who does not love his brother, whom he has seen, cannot love God, whom he has not seen" (1 John 4:20). You can't get around it: We must love. Anyone who does not love both God and people dares not take the name Christian.

LOVING ON TWO LEVELS

Love is an unequivocal command for the Christian, but love must be exercised on two different levels: love for God and love for people. It is important to understand that these two loves are not the same. Jesus differentiated between them in response to the question, "What is the greatest commandment?" He replied, "'Love the Lord your God with all your heart and with all your soul and with all your mind.' This is the first and greatest commandment. And the second is like it: 'Love your neighbor as yourself.' All the Law and the Prophets hang on these two commandments" (Matt. 22:37–40).

Our entire moral duty is summarized in these interwoven, two-directional commandments. Vertically, we are to love God with our whole selves. Horizontally, we are to love others as we love ourselves. The Ten Commandments in Exodus 20 are organized into the two directions of love. It is common to affirm that the first four commandments express the boundaries of our vertical love for God:

> You shall have no other gods before me.
> You shall not worship idols.
> You shall not misuse the name of the Lord your God.
> Remember the Sabbath day by keeping it holy.

Accordingly, the next six commandments express the boundaries of our horizontal love for others:

> Honor your father and your mother.
> You shall not murder.
> You shall not commit adultery.
> You shall not steal.
> You shall not give false testimony.
> You shall not covet.

The Ten Commandments spell out in greater detail what the two great commandments of Jesus summarize. Love for God implies obedience to the first four commandments. Love for people implies obedience to the last six commandments.

Notice that the first of the two great commandments of Christ has priority over the second. We are to love God with all our heart, soul, and mind—everything we are. We are to love others as we love ourselves. Do you see the difference? We are not to love people the way we love God. That would be blasphemous. Nor are we to love God the way we love people. God is to be loved *supremely*; people are to be loved *finitely*. God is absolute, ultimate, and infinite, and as such He demands ultimate love. People are only finite creatures made in the image of the infinite God, so our love for people is limited. This is not to say that our love should not be complete or of a high quality (see John 13:34) but that it is limited. In heaven our need for health, happiness, and growth will be completely filled in Christ's presence. We won't need the protection and provision of others, because Christ will be everything we need. But we will still enjoy the love and fellowship of one another.

So the Christian's love imperative is clearly segmented. We have two objects of love, and each is to be loved in a different way. To love God—to will His good—means to acknowledge His ultimate and supreme worth in all we think, say, and do. This is why Scripture calls us to worship God (worship was originally termed *worthship*). But no person should be the object of our worship as God is. That's idolatry. To love people—to will their good—means to recognize their value as persons created in God's image and treat them accordingly. The two levels of love are distinct and different.

How then are we to relate to the world God created for our use? God gave us animals, plants, and minerals to sustain life and to use in serving Him and others. God spoke the universe into existence and pronounced it "good" (Gen. 1:31). God's world is to be admired, enjoyed, cherished, protected, and utilized for our pleasure and His glory. We say we love the sight of a snow-capped mountain, a radiant sunset, a soaring hawk, a majestic cathedral, a playful kitten. But the material universe is not to be loved in the same way that we love God or people. If we esteem any *thing*—a house, a vehicle, artwork, a bank account, an animal, a career, a garden, anything—above God or people, we are mis-using God's creation; we are loving things in a way God did not intend. God is to be loved supremely, people are to be loved finitely, and God's creation is to be kept and protected in the service of God and others. This is the Christian love ethic in a nutshell.

WHEN LOVES CONFLICT

But now we have a problem. As we have seen, love for God and love for people are different. What are we to do when these two levels of love are in conflict? When our love for God, whom we are commanded to love, seemingly demands that we withhold love from a person we are also commanded to love, how should we respond? And when our love for a family member or friend demands that we withhold love from God, what should we do?

I (Norm) faced this conflict in a big way as a teenager. My parents were very antagonistic toward Christianity because of bitter hypocrisy they experienced in the church. So when I announced to them that I had become a Christian, I was con-fronted with strong opposition. Hoping to put a hasty end to the religious fanaticism she perceived in me, my mother threat-ened to kill me unless I gave up my faith. I was face to face with a crisis: Should I obey my parents and turn my back on God? Or should I put God first and disobey my parents? With God's help, I chose to obey God. My mother did not carry out her threat, obviously. But I received ridicule and criticism from my parents until, after several years of love and prayer, I was privileged to see both of them trust Christ as their Savior. God's Word is true: "Seek first his kingdom and his righteousness, and all these things will be given to you as well" (Matt. 6:33).

Some people have attempted to avoid the conflict by claiming that all love for God should be routed through people. They contend that we completely fulfill our obligation to love God when we love people. Two Scriptures are cited in support of this position. First, Jesus said, "Whatever you did for one of the least of these brothers of mine, you did for me" (Matt. 25:40). Second, John declared that we cannot love God if we do not love people (1 John 4:20). "There is no conflict," these people claim, "because the Bible clearly states that love for people constitutes love for God."

Whatever else these two verses imply, they do not teach that the only way to love God is to love Him through human beings. These verses do say two things. First, we cannot truly love God unless we also love people. Second, *one way* to love God is by loving people. Nowhere do the Scriptures teach that love for God can be expressed *only* by loving others.

How do we love God apart from loving people? C. S. Lewis contends that a large share of our love for God is what he terms *need-love*. As a helpless infant turns to its mother out of sheer need for comfort and safety, we love God because we are utterly dependent upon Him. Lewis writes, "Our whole being by its very nature is one vast need; incomplete, preparatory, empty yet cluttered, crying out for Him who can untie things that are now knotted together and tie up things that are still dangling loose."[1] We turn to God because we are helpless without His forgiveness, His support, His wisdom, and His consolation.

We may also express gift-love to God apart from our love for others. There is a sense in that we cannot give to God anything which is not already His. "But since it is only too obvious that we can withhold ourselves, our wills and hearts, from God, we can, in that sense, also give them,"[2] contends Lewis. We love God when we prayerfully offer Him our abilities and schedule at the beginning of the day. We love God whenever we sing His praise in church or in the sanctuary of our own heart. We love God whenever we turn off the TV in order to read Scripture or pray. We love God when we use our last wakeful moments to thank Him for His protection and provision through the day. In these very personal and often private expressions, we convey our love for God directly instead of through others.

Sometimes love for God, because it is primary, must take precedence over love for others. Consider Abraham, for example, to whom God said, "Take your son, your only son, Isaac, whom you love, and . . . sacrifice him . . . as a burnt offering" (Gen. 22:2). Abraham loved Isaac deeply. This was the son God had miraculously provided for him in his old age. But Abraham loved God supremely and would have sacrificed his son had God, satisfied at Abraham's display of obedience, not intervened at the last moment.

Jesus said, "If anyone comes to me and does not hate his father and mother, his wife and children, his brothers and sisters—yes, even his own life—he cannot be my disciple" (Luke 14:26). Jesus does not instruct us to hate family members here. He is using hyperbole to contrast the two great loves. Our love for God must be so much greater than our love for any human being—including those dearest to us—that our love for people will seem as hate compared to our love for God. We are to love God with all our heart, mind, soul, and strength. It would be an insult to God to love Him only as much as we love ourselves, which is how we are to love others. Jesus said, "If anyone would come after me, he must deny himself and take up his cross and follow me" (Matt. 16:24). God must be loved more than anyone else, including spouse, children, parents, dearest friends, and ourselves.

The two levels of love then are not always in harmony. There is often tension between them. For example, children are instructed, "Obey your parents in the Lord" (Eph. 6:1). But what happens when a parent instructs a Christian youth to give up his faith, curse God, or sin against God in some other way? Clearly, the child must disobey the parent. Obedience to parents is qualified by the phrase *in the Lord*, that is, only when the parent's instructions do not conflict with God's commandments. In such situations, love for the parent, whom the child is disobeying in order to obey God, may seem like hate to the parent.

The child must be certain, however, that the issue prompting disobedience to a parent is a clear violation of scriptural commands. For example, let's say that Jennifer, a Christian teenager, is prohibited by her unbelieving parents from dating Clint, a boy from her church. The order may be difficult for Jennifer to accept, but it does not violate any of God's commands. She must obey her parents on this. They may even prohibit her from attending church. This is a tough call, because Hebrews 10:25 states, "Let us not give up meeting together . . . but let us encourage one another." But Jennifer can still meet with other Christians at school, at parties, and in other places for mutual encouragement without actually attending church services.

However, if Jennifer's parents instruct her to tell a caller they are not home when they really are, falsify information on a college application to get more financial aid, or participate with them in a seance with some of their New Age friends, Jennifer has scriptural grounds to not obey them.

The same conflict between the two levels of love can be found in our relationship to authority. The New Testament strongly charges believers to express love for national, state, and local leaders by submitting to their authority. Peter writes, "Submit yourselves for the Lord's sake to every authority instituted among men" (1 Pet. 2:13). Paul adds, "Everyone must submit himself to the governing authorities. . . . He who rebels against the authority is rebelling against what God has instituted" (Rom. 13:1, 2). Submission clearly implies obedience, as seen in the interchangeable use of the words *submit* and *obey* when referring to our relationship to authorities. Paul wrote to Titus, "Remind the people to be subject to rulers and authorities, to be obedient, to be ready to do whatever is good" (Titus 3:1).

Yet there are times when loving loyalty and obedience to authorities clash with a Christian's supreme love and allegiance to God. The apostles found it necessary to disobey Jewish authorities and declare, "We must obey God rather than men!" (Acts 5:29). They were following in the footsteps of Old Testament believers who disobeyed human government with God's approval. The Hebrew midwives refused Pharaoh's command to kill all the male babies they helped deliver (Exod. 1). Daniel disobeyed Darius' ban on private prayer (Dan. 6), and his three companions Shadrach, Meshach, and Abednego defied Nebuchadnezzar's command to worship a golden image (Dan. 3). In each case, love for God transcended the command to obey human authorities.

Even though we may disagree at times with our national leaders, those of us living in free or democratic countries can be thankful that we are rarely pressed to choose between love for country and love for God. Christians in countries where faith is repressed and Judeo-Christian values are mocked are not as fortunate. Yet in our loving, respectful obedience to civil authorities, we may encounter situations where we cannot obey God *and* government. In those situations we must be prepared to love and obey God *rather* than government.

There are other arenas of life where love for God and love for people may come into conflict. A Christian wife may have an antagonistic husband who says, "I can't handle all this Christian stuff you're into. Take your choice. It's either Jesus or me." A shrewd boss may press a Christian employee to juggle company funds dishonestly, lie to clients, or compromise on safety standards. A staff member who must confront a Christian leader guilty of ongoing immorality will probably lose her job when the ministry of the defamed leader is disbanded.

Whenever the two great loves are in conflict, love for God must always take precedence over love for people. But even when we make the right choice, negative consequences may occur. Scripture and church history abound with accounts of individuals whose loving obedience to God cost them dearly. The author of Hebrews reports, "Some faced jeers and flogging, while still others were chained and put in prison. They were stoned; they were sawed in two; they were put to death by the sword. They went about in sheepskins and goatskins, destitute, persecuted and mistreated" (11:36, 37). Countless first-century Christians were fed to the lions because they loved God more than they loved the Roman emperor.

You likely will not face a love choice with life-and-death consequences. Your love for God, however, may cost you a job when you defy your boss's order to lie. You may be temporarily or permanently rejected by a friend, a parent, a child, or even a spouse for choosing the higher love. Such choices are not easy or pleasant. In these difficult choices and their painful consequences, we must cling to God's promise that "in all things God works for the good of those who love him, who have been called according to his purpose" (Rom. 8:28).

Love is absolute, but it isn't always simple. Normally, we face no real conflict between loving God and loving people. But sin often muddles the picture. Some people to whom we submit overstep their God-appointed domains and precipitate conflict for others by, in effect, playing God. Whenever a parent, political authority, employer, or spouse assumes sovereign power and demands ultimate allegiance, tension between the two levels of love results. In such forced options, the Christian must choose. And since God is of greater worth than any person, our love for Him must take precedence over love for anyone disputing His ultimate authority.

YIELDING TO A HIGHER AUTHORITY

When we must make a choice between loving God and loving others, it should not be regarded as breaking one commandment in order to keep another. For example, when Jennifer tells her parents that she will not lie on the financial aid form as they demand, she is not really breaking the fifth commandment. Rather, she is *suspending* and *transcending* the lower law in obedience to the higher law. Jennifer is not saying by her act that "honor your father and mother" doesn't apply to her. She is taking an exemption in view of her responsibility to love on a higher level.

It's similar to when a jetliner takes off, placing the laws of aerodynamics and gravity into conflict. As it lifts off, the aircraft doesn't break the law of gravity, it merely overpowers it for a time. Gravity is still in effect and will come into play again when the plane begins to decelerate. And Jennifer is committed to love and obey her parents in every area where their demands do not conflict with God's commands.

God has graded His moral laws so that some are higher than others. Jesus spoke of the "more important matters of the law" (Matt. 23:23). Paul identified love as the "greatest" virtue (1 Cor. 13:13). And Jesus spoke of the "great commandment" (Matt. 22:36). In effect, there is a pyramid of values: God at the pinnacle, people next, and things at the bottom. We are to love God more than people and people more than things. And when any two levels unavoidably conflict, we should always take the higher over the lower. God has built these signs into His moral law to help us know how to yield at a moment of conflict.

Loving God *more* than people doesn't necessarily mean that we love God *instead* of people. It's true that love for God may necessitate disobedience toward an intermediate authority, and this action may seem by contrast as hate. However, such a stand may be the best way to express our love for those whose directives conflict with God's. Love means giving to the sinner, not giving in to his or her sinful wishes. Love means willing a person's best, not a willingness to go along with his or her ungodly plans. Sometimes the best way to contribute to someone's good is to resist his or her evil. Passive resignation to evil is not a true expression of love for anyone. Therefore, in loving God more than others we are actually loving others more.

If you're a parent, you know that it's crazy to give your children everything they want. Your little ones may beg for cake and ice cream at every meal, insist on playing with the steak knives, or refuse to wear safety belts in the car. Your love is not diminished at all by denying those requests and requiring—

forcefully if necessary—compliance with your wishes. You know you have your children's best interests at heart whether they understand and accept it or not. Similarly, in your love for God, you may sometimes have to do seemingly hateful things to others in order to truly love them. Loving God the most helps us love others the best.

So the two levels of love may sometimes be in conflict, but they are never in contradiction. The lower law must be subordinated to the higher law but never completely disconnected from it. The highest expression of love for others is to will for them what God commands them to do. And God's command is the same for them as it is for you: that they take their place under God's loving, sovereign rule instead of usurping God's place in their lives.

When we turn to the command to love others, a new criterion comes into view. We are not to love people the way we love God. Rather, the definitive measure for the horizontal dimension of love is as up close and personal as the person in the mirror.

TOUGH QUESTIONS AND STRAIGHT ANSWERS ABOUT THE LOVE IMPERATIVE

Is it possible to love others and still stand up for your own rights?

If you are being clearly wronged in some way, the most loving thing you can do for the person wronging you is to stand up for what is right. Love is not tantamount to lying down so people can walk all over you. One of love's great strengths is to confront the wrong and make it right.

For example, you walk in the front door and find that your home has been looted and vandalized. Eventually the burglars are apprehended, but the stolen property is long gone. Some well-meaning Christians may counsel you, "Forgive them and drop all charges against them. It's the loving thing to do." Is such action in the best interest of the criminals? Wouldn't they be better served to feel the sting of the consequences for their actions? In your desire to express love for these people, you can at the same time forgive them for violating your home *and* press charges against them. You can befriend them, visit them in jail, and share Christ with them while cooperating with efforts to exact restitution from them.

For years I (Josh) thought I was doing the loving thing by rescuing some dear friends in the ministry from financial ruin. These people would launch out by faith into a project and soon flounder by mismanaging the funds that had been contributed to them. In their distress, they would call on me to bail them out. Touched by their plight, I would send them enough money to avert the collapse of the ministry. But within months they were in trouble again, and I would help them out again. The cycle continued for years.

Finally I realized that I was not doing my friends any favors by bailing them out of every financial scrape. In fact, my rescuing them was preventing them from learning the hard but necessary lessons of financial responsibility. I was actually doing the unloving thing by keeping them from these lessons. So I did one of the hardest things I've ever done: I quit bailing them out. I still love these friends dearly and pray for them constantly. But I am not only doing the loving thing, I am also doing the right thing.

LOVING THE PERSON IN THE MIRROR

8

Jesus has given us two great love commandments that summarize our prime responsibility to our Creator and our fellow humans: Love God, and love people. To love God is the higher law; to love people is the lower law. The two laws generally live in harmony. But whenever the two laws conflict, love for God must take precedence over love for people.

Each law was given with a qualifier to help us know *how* to love at each level. Jesus commanded us to love God "with all your heart and with all your soul and with all your mind" (Matt. 22:37). Love for God, the higher law, should permeate our thoughts, motives, choices, words, actions, and reactions. As for loving others, Jesus gave us a different but equally precise measuring device: "Love your neighbor as yourself" (v. 39). Paul's words in Ephesians 5:28 parallel Jesus' command: "Husbands ought to love their wives as their own bodies." Our love for others, Jesus' second greatest commandment, is to be patterned after our love for ourselves.

"Wait a minute!" someone may argue. "That's not biblical. We're not supposed to love ourselves. The Bible commands us to deny self and take up our cross. Jesus said if I love my life, I will lose it. It's like that acrostic J-O-Y: Jesus first, Others second, Yourself last. Self-love is right up there with pride and conceit, things we are to avoid."

On the contrary, proper self-love is right for at least three biblical reasons.

First, it is right to love ourselves because we are made in God's image (Gen. 1:26). We also love others for this reason, particularly certain individuals who seem lovable for no other reason. The unborn fetus, the seriously brain-damaged person, the unrepentant mass murderer, or the dying AIDS patient may contribute little or nothing to society. But we love them because they are God's creation. We must love ourselves for the same reason even in those discouraging moments when we don't feel we are worth loving.

Second, it is right to love ourselves because self-love is the basis for loving others. Had Jesus said, "Love others *instead* of loving yourself," we might conclude that any measure of self-love is wrong. But He commanded us to love others *as* we love ourselves. Self-love isn't commanded, it is assumed, implying that it is too basic to be included as a separate instruction. It's as if Jesus said, "You already love yourself, and to do so properly is good. Now love others the same way."

Third, it is right to love ourselves because God loves us (1 John 4:10). If we do not love ourselves, then we do not love what God loves, and it's never a good idea to oppose God.

The Christian's most basic earthly love obligation is to care for himself or herself. Paul understood that self-love was a given: "No one ever hated his own body, but he feeds and cares for it, just as Christ does the church" (Eph. 5:29). There are those words again: *feed* and *care for*, meaning nourish and cherish, provide and protect. It is normal and necessary for believers to nourish themselves to maturity mentally, physically, spiritually, and socially, and to protect themselves from harmful elements. This loving regard for ourselves is the pattern for our love for others.

It is difficult—if not impossible—to love others without loving yourself. Think of this in a purely human sense for a moment. A mall security guard who is grossly overweight and out of shape receives a call on his radio that a girl is being assaulted at the other end of the mall. The guard runs as fast as he can to help her, but his body isn't used to such a workout. Halfway to the emergency, the guard drops dead from a heart attack; the girl he might have saved is beaten to death. This man's neglect for himself cost him his life *and* resulted in another life lost. Had he cared about himself more, he may have lived to save the girl.

Likewise, self-love means learning how to swim, so you can save yourself and others; a non-swimmer can't help anyone in the water. Self-love means—as airline personnel instruct us before each flight—putting on your own oxygen mask before helping your child with his or her mask. If you don't put on your mask first, you may pass out, leaving your child without any help. Self-love means eating and exercising properly in order to extend your life for the sake of your children, grandchildren, and great-grandchildren. Self-love means working diligently to provide a living for yourself as well as to care for your family and to give to God's work. Self-love means investing time and effort in your own spiritual growth, so you are prepared to minister to others. In every area of loving and serving others, we cannot give what we do not have. Only as we love and care for ourselves are we equipped to love and care for others as Christ commanded us.

Self-love also means protecting ourselves mentally, physically, spiritually, and socially from harmful elements. Common safety measures, such as buckling up in the car, locking doors at night, keeping food and utensils clean, and avoiding substance abuse, are expressions of care and respect for our bodies. We lovingly protect our minds when we shun unwholesome reading material, TV programs, videos, music, and movies. Spiritually, we guard ourselves by filling our hearts with Scripture, holding ourselves accountable to others for spiritual growth, and standing against Satan's attempts to detour us from serving Christ. Caution and wisdom in the areas of self-protection are an expression of healthy self-love.

LOVING YOURSELF PROPERLY

As the objections mentioned earlier illustrate, Christians sometimes back away from self-love because of the stress laid on self-denial in Scripture and the warnings against selfishness. Jesus said, "If anyone comes to me and does not hate . . . even his own life—he cannot be my disciple" (Luke 14:26). Paul warned Timothy against people who are "lovers of themselves, lovers of money, boastful, proud" (2 Tim. 3:2). Paul confessed regarding his own human depravity, "I know that nothing good lives in me" (Rom. 7:18). Considering these and other references to self-denial, it may be difficult for some people to see self-love as part of the Christian love ethic.

Actually, these biblical instructions are in opposition not to loving ourselves but to *over*loving and *under*loving ourselves. We are to deny the selfishness and self-deprecation that occasionally assert themselves. But we are not to deny the self from which they come. It is our sin we should deny and despise, not the saint who is sometimes plagued by it.

Paul emphasized the inappropriateness of overloving and underloving ourselves in his instructions about spiritual gifts in 1 Corinthians 12. The apostle informs us that everyone is gifted by the Spirit for ministry (v. 7) and that God has equipped us just as He wants us to be (v. 18). He likens the body of Christ to a human body and each member to a body part: eye, ear, hand, foot, and so on. The straightforward lesson of the passage is that each of us is to accept the spiritual abilities God has given us and exercise them to the good of the body. That's proper self-love leading to the effective love of others.

Then Paul illustrated the wrong attitude of underloving ourselves: "If the foot should say, 'Because I am not a hand, I do not belong to the body,' it would not for that reason cease to be part of the body. And if the ear should say, 'Because I am not an eye, I do not belong to the body,' it would not for that reason cease to be part of the body" (vv. 15, 16). People like this don't love themselves enough. They whine, "I don't have much responsibility. I shouldn't be in the spotlight. I'm not important." They will have difficulty following through on Christ's command to love others because they are blocked from loving themselves by an inferiority complex or a false sense of self-denial.

For example, you probably love yourself too little if

- your spouse praises you for a good wall-papering job, but instead of saying thanks, you point out the flaws in your work

- a clerk cheats you out of a few cents in change but you fail to confront her on it because you don't want to make waves

- You are so involved in caring for your family and friends that you can't find any time for personal R and R

- You fail to give your opinion in an important discussion because you don't think it will make a difference

- You are overcommitted at church and stressed out at work because you feel guilty whenever you say no

This attitude of self-deprecation is contrasted with an equally wrong attitude on the other side of center. These people love themselves too much. They overestimate their importance to God and to others. Pride and self-absorption will hinder them in their efforts to fulfill Christ's command to love others. Paul wrote of such people, "The eye cannot say to the hand, 'I don't need you!' And the head cannot say to the feet, 'I don't need you!'" (v. 21).

For example, you probably love yourself too much if

- you can't pull yourself away from TV to help a distraught neighbor search for a runaway dog

- the things you want to do consistently keep you from accomplishing the things you should do

- success at work or enjoyment of your hobbies is more important to you than your responsibilities as a spouse or a parent

- you dominate discussions because you're convinced no one else has the informed perspective you have on the topic

- you break commitments at home, at work, or at church when you become bored or receive a better offer

Think of yourself as a basketball. Your whole purpose for existence is to represent the sport that bears your name and bring enjoyment to those you were created to serve. But if you are overinflated, you will bounce too high and shots will ricochet wildly off the backboard. If you are underinflated, you won't bounce. Either way, the game will suffer and the participants' enjoyment will be hampered. The right amount of pressure makes all the difference in your success. If you had the capability, you would do everything you could to keep yourself properly inflated—not too much air, not too little.

Similarly, if we undervalue or overvalue ourselves, we are less fit to love others as Christ has commanded us. Failing to properly love and provide for yourself leaves you with a very low reservoir of love to share with others. You will burn out fast and often. You will also run dry in your love for others if you lavish most of your love energy on yourself. It is a healthy, balanced self-love and a respectful attention to nourishing ourselves to maturity and protecting ourselves from damaging influences that best equips us to love others as we love ourselves.

It is not self-love that is wrong; it is why some people love themselves that is wrong. To love ourselves simply for the sake of loving ourselves can be sinful. But to love ourselves for the sake of loving others is definitely good. The pilot who gets enough rest and avoids alcohol loves himself for the sake of his passengers. The pregnant mother who eats properly and refrains from using alcohol and other drugs loves her body for the sake of her baby. The Bible study leader who studies and prays thoroughly for his own spiritual growth loves himself for the sake of his study group. The Christian who memorizes key

Bible verses on evangelism loves herself for the sake of those she may eventually lead to Christ. To provide for ourselves as God's beloved creation is good; loving ourselves selfishly as though God's creation revolved around us is a most basic evil (Rom. 1:25). Christian balance is having a proper, sound estimate of oneself (Rom. 12:3).

TOUGH QUESTIONS AND STRAIGHT ANSWERS ABOUT SELF-LOVE

Jesus said, "Greater love has no one than this, that he lay down his life for his friends" (John 15:13). How can we love ourselves and still sacrifice ourselves for others as this verse suggests?

Self-love and self-sacrifice are not contradictory concepts. In reality, it's only when we love ourselves that we can really give ourselves to others in love. Without a proper love for self, we don't have the needed love reserve to sacrifice for others. Certainly those who love themselves too much will be reticent to risk personal comfort, let alone life, for the sake of another. And the sacrifice of those who love themselves too little is likely driven by guilt instead of by love. Only those who are at peace with themselves through proper self-love are free to see the needs of others and make sacrifices to serve them. A mother who risks her life by donating a kidney to a child dying of kidney failure does not hate her own life. She loves herself so much that she wants to share her very life with her child.

How does a Christian get rid of an inferiority complex that keeps him or her from healthy self-love?

The most direct route to a healthy self-image and proper self-love is to see yourself through the eyes of the God who

loves you. If you are a Christian, you have nothing to feel inferior about. Saturate yourself with scriptural truth about your
identity in Christ. For example:

- God loves you and gave His Son for you (1 John 4:10).

- You are a child of God (John 1:12; Rom. 8:14–15).

- Christ calls you His friend (John 15:15).

- God's Spirit lives in you (1 Cor. 3:16, 6:19).

- You are brand-new in Christ (2 Cor. 5:17).

- God has made you righteous in Christ (Eph. 4:24).

- You are in the light, not in the darkness (1 Thess. 5:5).

- You are God's workmanship (Eph. 2:10).

The more thoroughly you internalize the truth about who
you are in Christ, the more you will be able to love yourself as
God does.

How can I love myself when I continue to sin?

Christians with a healthy self-love understand that they're
not perfect. But they don't give up on themselves and say,
"What's the use? I'm never going to get it together spiritually."
They understand that they are called not to sin, but that when
they do sin, Christ is their advocate with the Father to help
them make things right and go on (1 John 2:1). They continue
to work on growing in their faith and correcting the patterns
that lead to sin. As Christians, we're not always what we ought
to be, but by the grace of God neither are we what we used to
be. And as we press on toward maturity, we are in the process
of becoming what God wants us to be.

When you sin, don't give in to it and don't give up on yourself.

Confess your sin, receive God's forgiveness, and keep growing. Perfection is our ultimate goal, but we won't reach it until we get to heaven. Don't get down on yourself every time you realize you're not perfect yet. Our intermediate goal is maturity, and we can succeed at that in some way every day.

LOVING NEIGHBORS FAR AND NEAR

9

J esus made it clear that the command to love our neighbor is not limited to our care for the person who lives next door. The word may be singular but the moral intent is plural. God wants us to love all our neighbors because He loves all our neighbors. When Jesus was asked, "Who is my neighbor?" He told the parable of the Good Samaritan, who exercised love toward a man in need (Luke 10:29–37). The story clearly illustrates that neighbors are not limited to people in certain classes, geographical locations, or socioeconomic strata. Neighbors are people in need, whoever and wherever they are. And those who are neighborly—that is, loving—help people in need. Neighbors are, in a sense, all people everywhere, for everyone needs to be loved.

Jesus' command that believers must love everyone was not new. Old Testament Jews knew about God's love for all people and His will that they love as He does. God chose Abraham to be the father of the Hebrew family so that through him and his descendants "all peoples on earth will be blessed" (Gen. 12:3). Moses, not Jesus, was the first to hear and write in the law God's words, "Love your neighbor as yourself" (Lev. 19:18). God commanded Israel to show loving concern not only for those of their own kind but also for the poor and strangers (Lev. 19:9–10) and to seek peace with their enemies whenever possible (Deut. 20:10–12). Jonah discovered that God loved even the wicked Assyrians (Jon. 4:2). God's invitation permeates the Old Testament: "Love people— all people—as I do."

In the New Testament, God's love is offered to all people. Christ died for the whole world (John 3:16), and we are to share the good news of salvation with "all nations" (Matt. 28:19). Christians are commanded, "As we have opportunity, let us do good to all people" (Gal. 6:10). Our love is not to be limited to people like us and people we like. Jesus instructed, "Love your enemies, do good to those who hate you, bless those who curse you, pray for those who mistreat you" (Luke 6:27–28). He left no loopholes in the love command. Love is comprehensive. All people must be loved for Christ's sake. Everyone is our neighbor in the broadest sense of the word.

LOVING OTHERS COMPREHENSIVELY

In a more particular sense, our neighbor is the person at hand, the one whose need for love is near. This is extremely important to the Christian love ethic because we cannot literally love all people. We don't have sufficient time, energy, or resources to care for everyone everywhere. If we tried, our love would be spread so thin over so many that it would not mean very much to any. That's why the Bible gives us what may be called the principle of centralized loving. We are to fulfill the command to love people by starting with those closest to us and working out to the whole world "as we have opportunity" (Gal. 6:10).

The inner circle of the Christian's love responsibility, as we have already discussed, is ourself. If we do not take care to provide for our basic needs and protect ourselves from damaging influences, we will not be able to love others effectively. Regarding care for ourselves, Paul wrote, "Make it your ambition to lead a quiet life, to mind your own business and to work with your hands, just as we told you, so that your daily life may win the respect of outsiders and so that you will not be dependent on anybody" (1 Thess. 4:11–12); "Each one should carry his own load" (Gal. 6:5). In other words, it's up to each of us to provide for our own life needs in order to not be a burden to others and to have something to share with people in need. Furthermore, we are responsible for our own spiritual nurture and growth. We must love ourselves enough to schedule consistent time in the Scriptures, prayer, and Christian fellowship. Each person is responsible for growing mentally, emotionally, and socially. If we don't maintain this inner circle of self-love, we are ill-equipped to move on to the outer circles of people God has called us to love.

Next to properly loving self, our most immediate love responsibility is to love our own families. God's answer to Cain's famous question, "Am I my brother's keeper?" (Gen. 4:9) is a resounding yes. Paul wrote plainly on this point, "If anyone does not provide for his relatives, and especially for his immediate family, he has denied the faith and is worse than an unbeliever" (1 Tim. 5:8). Jesus came down hard on religious leaders who ignored basic loving care for their parents (Mark 7:10–13). A man and woman joined in marriage are "one flesh" (Gen. 2:24). The children they produce are an extension of that union, making family-love a very natural and necessary extension of self-love.

Even though each individual is responsible to care for himself or herself, no one is a self-sustaining island of total independence (Rom. 14:7). Everyone needs the assistance, encouragement, prayer, comfort, and counsel of others at times. We are obligated under God to fill these needs for family members. Providing for and protecting spouse, children, parents, and siblings is our first priority in response to the second great commandment to love others. Caring for extended family, such as grandparents, aunts, uncles, and cousins, is a close but lesser priority (1 Tim. 5:16).

If family vacations, date nights with your spouse, or a child's soccer game are the last items to be penciled into your calendar—or first to be erased—because you're too busy, you may need to rethink God's priorities for loving others. If work commitments leave you too tired for quality conversation and prayer with your spouse, you're working too hard. If you're too busy with church activities to help a child with homework or assist an aging parent with a household repair, you're too busy at church. Our first love commitment must be to those closest to us who need us, those of our own family.

The next sphere of love is to our fellow believers in need. Paul urged, "Therefore, as we have opportunity, let us do good to all people, *especially to those who belong to the family of believers*" (Gal. 6:10, emphasis added). Christians are to love all people, but we have a priority responsibility to those who share our faith. John added, "If anyone has material possessions and sees his brother in need but has no pity on him, how can the love of

God be in him?" (1 John 3:17). Protecting and providing for the needs of our brothers and sisters in the faith is a high-priority expression of our love.

Outside the circle of the family, your first concern should be the company of believers with whom you worship, learn, serve, and fellowship. At this level you may find your small group (a neighborhood or campus Bible study, a care group, a support group), your Sunday school class, your ministers and church congregation, your close Christian friends, your parachurch ministry team, and other Christians with whom you interact regularly. Another level may include believers you don't know as well: denomination leaders, members of sister congregations, missionaries, outreach organizations. At the outer reaches of this category are Christians you do not know and will likely never meet: believers in other denominations, cities, and countries.

Loving one another as Christ commanded is the heartbeat of our relationship with other Christians. But sometimes we place too much emphasis on love within the body of Christ. Just like any group of people with an affinity by reason of belief, history, or activity, Christians find it relatively easy to love one another. The real test comes in loving those who are least like us—worldly people, unlovely people, hateful people. We seem to spend an inordinate amount of time discussing how to protect and provide for one another, leaving pitiful little time for instructing and encouraging ourselves in loving the world.

Furthermore, we are sometimes so busy teaching and fellowshiping with one another that we don't leave much time for interacting with our unbelieving neighbors and coworkers. As someone insightfully observed, "We are so heavenly minded that we're no earthly good." Two or three church services, a committee meeting or two, choir practice, a teacher training meeting, a men's or women's fellowship group, and an all-church work day can fill up a week. All of these activities are good, but if they keep us from getting together with our unbelieving neighbors or coworkers, Christian love for fellow believers may be too much of a good thing.

Beyond the circles of family and faith lies "all people" whom we are to love as we love ourselves. This expansive category ranges from your literal neighbors, schoolmates, and coworkers to remote tribes you have never heard about. Whoever and wherever they are, we are to love them.

Like a pebble cast into the water, the main thrust of love will be at the center of its responsibility, to those nearest—family and fellow believers. But the ripples must continue to flow outward. As Paul wrote, "If it is possible, as far as it depends on you, live at peace with everyone" (Rom. 12:18). Peace is a kindred virtue to love. Wherever you go in the world outside the inner circles of family and faith, your love for others will be an avenue for peace.

There is an important implication to this concept of centralized loving: When there is a conflict as to who should be loved and how much, those closest to the center of our love responsibility take priority over those farther out. Here are a few stark examples: A mother should not give the last of the food to the hungry neighbor children when her own children have not been fed. Nor is a father obligated to buy clothes for the poor in Third World countries if his own family is without clothes. A person will rescue his or her family members and friends from a burning building before helping others.

On a more practical, day-to-day level, a Christian man should make sure he is spending enough time with his wife and children before he commits time to his church responsibilities.

And the men in his Bible study group should come ahead of the guys on his bowling team. A single career woman with limited funds will regard the needs of her unemployed parents ahead of her church's building campaign and local drive for the cancer fund. A pastor pours his prime energy into nurturing his flock instead of evangelizing outside the circle of his congregation.

In most cases, love will not be an either–or choice but a both–and distribution based on the concentric circles of priority. Parents whose children are adequately fed and clothed will share their excess with others in need. A man may allocate prime time to his devotional life and family responsibilities while saving one night a week for Bible study, one night a month for committee meetings, and two nights a month for bowling league. The career woman may designate 70 percent of her limited discretionary income to help her parents while giving 20 percent to the building fund and 10 percent to cancer research. Love's obligation begins at home and then should spread out as far as possible. Within each circle, necessities should be met before the surplus overflows to the next level. In this way the ripples from the many centers of love will reach out to the otherwise unloved ones outside these centers.

Each individual must discern between needs and wants at each level of centralized loving. For example, your children may want you to spend three hours every night of the week helping them with homework and playing with them. But you know that an hour a night or two full evenings a week is sufficient for quality interaction and help. This allows you to meet the needs of others you choose to love with your time and attention: your spouse, your Bible study group, your bowling team. As a single adult with a big job promotion, you may be itching to move into a larger apartment in a complex with the recreation facilities and conveniences you've always wanted. But you know you can get by comfortably where you are, freeing more funds to help your parents and to increase your giving to the overseas orphanage you help support.

Love wills and works for the good of the persons loved, but it doesn't mean being extravagant at one level and miserly at another. Love requires us to be observant and resourceful in order to discern genuine needs so that the surplus of centralized loving can flow out as far as possible and touch as many people as possible.

This principle of centralized loving is evident in both the love of Christ and His last words to the disciples. Jesus spent most of His time teaching a small group of men, His inner circle. Then there was the group of seventy He sent out two-by-two. There were hundreds and perhaps thousands more that He taught on the mountainside and the seashore. His entire ministry took place in His homeland and was directed largely to His own people, the Jews. Yet the surplus of His love flowed out to many others, such as Syrophenicians, Samaritans, Gadarenes, and Romans. Some Greeks asked Jesus to minister to their people, but they were informed that His ministry to Jerusalem had priority (John 12:20ff). The gospel would spread to Greece later. Even after Jesus rose from the grave, He said that the ministry should begin at home in Jerusalem and Judea, spread to neighboring territories such as Samaria, and out to the rest of the world (Acts 1:8). Jesus taught and modeled that love for all happens best when love for those we are nearest to comes first.

LOVING OTHERS COMPLETELY

Love should not only be comprehensive but also complete. The Christian love ethic demands that we love the whole of humanity and the whole person, not just the eternal soul. In Jesus' parable, the Good Samaritan didn't preach to the wounded man about his eternal destiny, he bound up his wounds and transported him to an inn to be cared for. Jesus not only spoke to people about the "bread of life" to fill their spiritual hunger (John 6:35), but He also gave them physical bread for their physical hunger (John 6:5–11). Every individual is a whole person, a unity of soul and body, and these parts are equally valuable to God. God made us one in essence even as He is one in nature (Deut. 6:4). The doctrine of the resurrection of the saints doesn't make any sense if we are complete without our physical bodies (2 Cor. 5:1–6).

Since every person is an inseparable unit, it is not unusual that the commands of love address the whole person, not just the soul. John made this unmistakably clear when he wrote, "If anyone has material possessions and sees his brother in need but has no pity on him, how can the love of God be in him?" (1 John 3:17). James was equally emphatic: "Suppose a brother or sister is without clothes and daily food. If one of you says to him, 'Go, I wish you well; keep warm and well fed,' but does nothing about his physical needs, what good is it? In the same way, faith by itself, if it is not accompanied by action, is dead" (James 2:15–17). For example, in a skid row rescue mission where caring people distribute "soup and salvation" to the destitute of the streets, the soup is as much an expression of Christ's love as the message of salvation. The watching world is not impressed by our passion to save souls if we neglect obvious physical needs.

Be assured that you are obeying Christ's command to love others as much when you donate money to a disaster relief fund as when you give an offering to an evangelistic outreach ministry. A hundred-pound sack of potatoes given to a homeless shelter is as much an expression of love as the Sunday school lesson you serve to your class. Admittedly, food, clothing, and shelter alone don't bring people into the kingdom of God. They must also hear the good news about Christ and trust Him as Savior and Lord. But it's difficult to listen to a Bible lesson or a testimony when your stomach is knotted with hunger or your broken body aches from injuries suffered during an earthquake. Loving care for physical needs opens the door for the meeting of spiritual needs. The late Henrietta Mears noted, "Kindness has converted more sinners than zeal, eloquence, or learning."

Ministries that seek to provide basic physical needs and feed spiritual hunger offer a double helping of the love of Christ. One such ministry is Operation Carelift, a facet of the Josh McDowell Ministry and Campus Crusade for Christ International. Since 1992, Operation Carelift has utilized thousands of volunteers annually to collect, pack, and deliver food, clothing, medical supplies, and school supplies to the destitute citizens of Russia. Careboxes, carebags, and hungerboxes are delivered in person by hundreds of Carelift volunteers. And with the supplies come Bibles, copies of *More Than a Carpenter*, and the gospel message. One director of a Russian school said of the Carelift workers, "They must be from another planet, and that planet must be love!" When a Russian teacher learned that the volunteers had paid their own way to bring these gifts from America to her country, her eyes filled with tears. "That's real love," she said.

Another Christian organization, Northwest Medical Teams, headquartered in Portland, Oregon, mobilizes volunteer physicians and nurses to serve the sick and injured in areas where drought, war, devastating floods, and killer earthquakes have taken a human toll. Lifesaving medical care given in love opens spiritually blind eyes to the love of Christ. Samaritan's Purse, operated by Billy Graham's son, Franklin, helps needy people all over the world, as do World Vision and many others.

Our responsibility as Christians to love the whole person goes beyond the basic needs of food, clothes, and medical care. People also have social needs. In His parable about caring for hurting people, Jesus spoke of loneliness when He said, "I was a stranger and you invited me in, . . . I was in prison and you came to visit me" (Matt. 25:35–36). James urged us to "look after orphans and widows in their distress" (James 1:27). Visiting or corresponding with elderly shut-ins, AIDS patients, or prison inmates is an expression of love in action. So is seeking out church members, neighbors, or coworkers who are shunned by others or telephoning a hurting friend just to listen and let her know that you are there for her. In situations like these, it is the gifts of time and attention that convey our love.

Another situation in which love can be effectively activated is oppression. Referring to the Israelites enslaved in Egypt, God demanded of Pharaoh, "Let my people go." Oppression of all kinds is forbidden by God. "Do not mistreat an alien or oppress him. . . . Do not take advantage of a widow or an orphan" (Exod. 22:21–22). Whenever you act to correct racial injustice, whenever you vote in favor of a ballot measure that protects the God-given rights of an individual or group, whenever you confront an employer over unfair treatment of workers, you are expressing love to the victims of oppression. It is the responsibility of Christian love to oppose oppression and work for the good of all people. Love is equally concerned about physical needs, social needs, and spiritual needs.

TOUGH QUESTIONS AND STRAIGHT ANSWERS ABOUT
LOVING OTHERS

How can we love Christians who are living in sin?

Love provides what people need and protects them from harm. Disobedient Christians need to be lovingly confronted with their disobedience in hopes of protecting them from the consequences of their wrong behavior. For example, you have a single Christian friend who is sleeping with her boyfriend. She needs someone to say, "In light of God's purity and the Bible's clear declaration that sexual immorality is wrong, I challenge you to stop sleeping with him." She might not want to hear it, but you are acting in your friend's best interest. Love seeks to protect her from a burden of remorse in a future marriage and possible sexually transmitted diseases.

Some people call this "tough love," risking a relationship in order to turn a fellow Christian away from sin. You do people no favors by glossing over their behavior in order to spare their feelings or salvage your relationship. They are in much greater danger if they continue in the wrong direction. The people you confront may not listen to you, and they may walk out of your life for a while or for good. Exercising love comes with no guarantees that your efforts will be received. You can only do your best under God to provide for their good and protect them from harm. How they respond is up to them and God.

How can we love unbelievers whose values and behaviors conflict with Christian values and behaviors?

In your thinking, you have to separate the sinner from the sinful behavior. Love the sinner as a person God loves, then deal with the sin. Love provides and protects. Unbelievers have genuine physical, emotional, and spiritual needs. Provide for their needs without compromising your faith as you have opportunity. Then share Christ with them, seeking to protect them from the ultimate harm they face: eternity without God.

For example, you have a coworker who is flagrantly racist in his remarks and behaviors. As much as his lifestyle may repulse you, this is a person for whom Christ died. He is not headed for hell because he is a racist; his behavior is a symptom of his need for Christ. Look for ways to be a positive influence and encouragement to him, just as you would for anyone else in your office or shop. Do what you can to do what is best for him. Pray that God will give you opportunities that will turn his life from sin and his heart to Christ.

LAYING DOWN THE LAW OF LOVE 10

Many years ago I (Josh) was invited to appear on John Ankerberg's television talk show to debate Anson Mount, cofounder with Hugh Hefner of the Playboy philosophy. The topic of debate was love, morals, and ethics. It sounded like a great opportunity to share Christ, so I eagerly accepted the invitation. I didn't realize what I was getting myself into.

As I prepared for the program, I began to get nervous. I knew the topic of situation ethics—which suggests that in every moral situation we must do the loving thing—would come up because the Playboy philosophy is largely based upon it and my opponent was a firm advocate of it. Mount even quotes Romans 13:8: "Let no debt remain outstanding, except the continuing debt to love one another, for he who loves his fellowman has fulfilled the law." I was getting nervous because I believed the same way: We must do the loving thing in every situation. I couldn't find a nugget of difference between my position and what I expected to hear from Anson Mount.

As the days dwindled down to the debate, the nervousness in my heart grew to panic. I have never been so afraid of facing a topic or a speaking engagement in more than thirty years of ministry. I studied Romans 13:8 in commentary after commentary trying to find a flaw in situation ethics. Everything I read agreed that doing the loving thing is biblical, and I didn't see how the Playboy philosophy could be wrong if it agreed with the Bible. I was going on national television representing Christianity, and I wouldn't have an answer to the Playboy philosophy. I just knew I was already dead and buried as a defender of the faith.

The night before the debate I locked myself in my hotel room with my Bible, determined to find the answer. Every so often my wife Dottie would call and ask, "Did you find it yet?"

"No," I'd say, "but keep praying."

Eventually I got back to reading Romans 13:8. But instead of stopping with that one verse, I read on to verses 9 and 10. The answer came like a lightning bolt in these words: "The commandments, 'Do not commit adultery,' 'Do not murder,' 'Do not steal,' 'Do not covet,' and whatever other commandment there may be, are summed up in this one rule: 'Love your neighbor as yourself.' Love does no harm to its neighbor. Therefore love is the fulfillment of the law." Situation ethics says, "Do the loving thing," but it doesn't tell you what the loving thing is. That's like being in the middle of the Pacific Ocean with no navigational aids and being told to sail to San Francisco. God says, "Do the loving thing," and then He tells how to love in His commandments, including the clear command regarding sexual behavior: "Do not commit adultery." God did not leave us adrift to figure out the loving thing based on the situation; He gave us specific direction. His law of love does not eliminate His commandments; it merely summarizes them. God's laws are a compass and sextant that point us to specific loving behavior by proscribing unloving behavior. If you love someone, you won't harm him or her: You will seek only what is best for that person.

I called Dottie and we rejoiced together over God's timely help. The debate went well. I apparently didn't change Anson Mount's mind about the immorality of the Playboy philosophy, but I trust that God used my presentation to speak to thousands of viewers that evening.

A lot of people today believe what I once wrongly assumed: that love and law are incompatible. They contend that people in the Old Testament were under law while people from the New Testament on—including Christians today—are under grace or love. John 1:17 and Romans 6:14 are often quoted in support of this view: "For the law was given through Moses; grace and truth came through Jesus Christ"; "You are not under law, but under grace." But it is not either law *or* love; it is the law of love. That's why David could say with joy, "Oh, how I love your law! . . . I love your commands more than gold, more than pure gold" (Ps. 119:97, 127).

While it is true that Christians are not under either the ceremonies or curses of the Mosaic law (Heb. 8–10; Gal. 3:13), the ethical principles embodied in the Mosaic law are still binding on Christians. In reality, the eternal ethical principles expressed in the Ten Commandments are not incompatible with the nature of God as love; they are in fact an expression of that love. In the two greatest commandments—love God and love people—God tells us to do the loving thing. In the Ten Commandments and other instructions in the Bible, God shows us what the loving thing is and warns us against the unloving thing.

LAYING DOWN THE LAW IN THE OLD TESTAMENT

Love is the foundation of the Mosaic law. The opening words of the Ten Commandments are an expression of God's love for His people: "I am the Lord your God, who brought you out of Egypt, out of the land of slavery" (Exod. 20:2). This statement is one of the most prominent truths in all the Old Testament, appearing in some form at least one hundred times. It reminded Israel of God's most celebrated act of love for them: deliverance from oppression in Egypt. The introduction to the second commandment further emphasizes God's love: "I, the Lord your God . . . showing love to a thousand generations of those who love me and keep my commandments" (Exod. 20:5–6). Descriptive words for God, such as mercy, kindness, goodness, and favor, abound in the Old Testament. Whoever originated the error that love is exclusively a New Testament teaching was not reading the Old Testament.

The very law itself is an expression of God's love. We see in the Ten Commandments God's commitment to provide for us and protect us from harm. The fifth commandment includes a loving promise: "Honor your father and your mother, so that you may live long in the land the Lord your God is giving you" (Exod. 20:12). Other laws often include a phrase like, "So that the Lord your God may bless you in all the work of your hands" (Deut. 14:29). After reading the law to the Israelites from Mount Gerizim, Moses reminded them, "All these blessings will come upon you and accompany you if you obey the Lord your God: You will be blessed in the city and blessed in the country. The fruit of your womb will be blessed, and the crops of your land and the young of your livestock—the calves of your herds and the lambs of your flocks. Your basket and your kneading trough will be blessed. You will be blessed when you come in and blessed when you go out" (Deut. 28:2–6). In his farewell speeches to Israel, Moses exhorted, "Carefully follow the terms of this covenant, so that you may prosper in everything you do" (Deut. 29:9).

When God gave the law, He said it was "for your own good" (Deut. 10:13), to provide for us and protect us. God's purpose in giving His law was to bless His people by providing for our prosperity and joy and to protect us from heartache and hurt. The curses in the law are simply warnings for those who do not keep the law. How loving God is to give people plenty of advance warning in hopes of sparing them from the consequences of sin! God's laws spell out the loving course of action in our relationship to God and people. They are given to help us fulfill the two great commandments. The written law is love stated in words.

LAYING DOWN THE LAW IN THE NEW TESTAMENT

The vital importance of the law did not diminish with the dawn of the New Testament. Jesus declared, "Do not think that I have come to abolish the Law or the Prophets; I have not come to abolish them but to fulfill them" (Matt. 5:17). More than ninety times Jesus and the New Testament writers affirm "it is written," citing the Old Testament as the authority for their teaching.

Nine of the Ten Commandments are repeated in the New

Testament, most of them almost verbatim. Paul underscores prohibitions of adultery, murder, stealing, and coveting in Romans 13:8 and 9. Honoring parents is found in Ephesians 6:2. Idolatry is condemned in many places (Gal. 5:19–20; 1 John 5:21), as is lying (Eph. 4:25). Swearing is condemned by Jesus in Matthew 5:34, and the supremacy of God is affirmed in several places, such as 1 Corinthians 8:5 and 6. Only the Sabbath or seventh day law was not repeated. The early Christians worshiped on the first day of the week (Acts 20:7) or "Lord's Day" (Rev. 1:10), the day Christ rose from the dead (Matt. 28:1). The majority of Christians today hold that the Sabbath day law was fulfilled in Christ's resurrection. Some Christians believe that the spirit of setting aside one day in seven for worship and rest is preserved in the New Testament "Lord's day."

So we can't put the Ten Commandments on the shelf by arguing that love replaced law in the New Testament. The commandments were as important to New Testament believers as to Old Testament believers. The New Testament command to love God and love people may *summarize* the Ten Commandments, but it is not a *substitute* for them. God's laws provide practical guidance for fulfilling God's command to love.

So if the moral principles behind the Ten Commandments were not abolished in the New Testament, in what sense are Christians today "not under law, but under grace" (Rom. 6:14)? A key passage to answering this question is Galatians 3:13: "Christ redeemed us from the curse of the law by becoming a curse for us." We are no longer under the curse of the moral law of Moses because Christ paid the penalty for all law breaking. Christ took the curse of sin, which is death, the penalty for disobeying the law, upon Himself (1 Cor. 15:55–56). But taking away the curse of the law and abolishing the moral principles embedded in its commands are two different matters.

Since the Ten Commandments are restated in the New Testament, these moral principles of the law are still binding on Christians. But the context of the law is grace instead of judgment since Christ took the judgment for our sin on Himself. It is the same moral law, only the curses are not attached. For example, the judgment for adultery in the Old Testament was death (Lev. 20:10). Adultery is still prohibited in the New Testament, but no such penalty is included. Why? Because Christ paid the death penalty for all sin, including adultery. In the early church, Paul instructed that an adulterer be removed from the church for discipline (1 Cor. 5:1–5) and then restored and comforted (2 Cor. 2:5–8). The commandment is the same, but the curse, having been paid, has been removed and a blessing is promised for those who repent and receive the cleansing that Christ's death purchased.

The moral curse of the law may be gone, but be assured that sin still carries physical and emotional consequences. Adultery inflicts heartbreak on the offended families, guilt on the participants, and shame on the church or community. Christian marriages have been ruined and ministries blighted by adultery. Furthermore, the adulterer, though penitent and forgiven, may have to live with a divorce, an unplanned child, or sexually transmitted disease as a result of disobedience. Sin always exacts a toll, but thanks to God's grace, the eternal curse has been paid by Christ.

Not only are the curses of the law abolished in the New Testament, but the blessings are also changed. For example, the Old Testament blessing for honoring parents was "that you may live long in the land the Lord your God is giving you"

(Exod. 20:12). When the command is restated in Ephesians 6:3, the blessing promised is "that it may go well with you and that you may enjoy long life on the earth." The same is true of other commandments. The *content* of the New Testament moral commands is identical to that of the Old Testament, but the *context* is different. One is a Mosaic context applied to a theocratic nation; the other is applied to individual believers. One has specific sanctions and blessings not applicable to the other.

The similarity between the moral law in the Old and New Testaments can be illustrated by a civil law that is the same in two different countries. For example, breaking the speed limit is as much a violation in the United Kingdom as it is in the United States. But just because you are caught speeding in Los Angeles doesn't mean you have broken the law in London. It's the same law but in two different countries. The eternal ethical principles embodied in the Mosaic law are the same ones restated in the New Testament, but the context is grace instead of judgment, since the judgment has been paid by Christ. If you commit adultery under grace, you have violated God's law, but you won't have to pay with your life as if you lived under the Mosaic law 3,000 years ago. Christ paid with His life once for all (Heb. 10:10). That's why John wrote, "The law was given through Moses; grace and truth came through Jesus Christ" (John 1:17). By grace, Christ took the curse of Moses' law on Himself. By grace through faith in His atoning death, that curse is removed from us.

Christians are not under Moses' particular codification of the Ten Commandments. We live in a different "country." When we lie or steal, we are not breaking Moses' law nor do we pay the consequences of Moses' law. Christians who lie or steal are breaking God's eternal law, which was originally embodied in the Ten Commandments and is an expression of the very nature and character of God Himself. We are, however, bound to God's law by virtue of its expression in the New Testament, apart from the national and theocratic characteristics that were unique to Israel.

God has not changed (Heb. 6:18, 13:8). He is still the God of love in the New Testament as He was in the Old Testament. And the moral principles that express His love to us and show us how to express it to God and others are still the same.

LAW AND LOVE IN HARMONY

Whenever we talk about following laws to express the love of God and our love for God and others, somebody invariably confronts us with the charge of "legalism." In the eyes of some people, anyone who reveres the Ten Commandments is a modern-day Pharisee. But are laws and love incompatible? Are we necessarily legalistic because we believe in many universally binding moral laws? The New Testament gives a clear answer to these questions: no.

Jesus never replaced the laws of Moses with a single law of love as some have suggested. First of all, Jesus never said that there was only one law of love. He spoke of at least two: one for loving God and one for loving people (Matt. 22:37–39). Furthermore, Jesus never said these were to be *substituted* for the many moral laws embodied in the Old Testament; they were merely a *summary* of them. Jesus said He came to fulfill the law, not to abolish it (Matt. 5:17). Likewise, the apostle John wrote, "I am not writing you a new command but an old one, which you have had since the beginning. . . . This is the message you heard from the beginning: We should love one another" (1 John 2:7, 3:11). The love commandments do not replace the Ten Commandments; they only reduce them to their common essence: love. Why? Because if we love God and our fellow man, we will not break God's commandments (Rom. 13:10). The two commandments of love merely summarize (i.e., fulfill the purpose of) the many moral laws. All of the many laws depend on love as their foundation and are fulfilled by love in their manifestation. Law and love are not incompatible; they fit like hand and glove.

Each of the Ten Commandments gives us the loving thing to do and the unloving thing to avoid in our relationship with God and others. Each law is love put into words that guide us into concrete, loving courses of action.

1. *You shall have no other gods before me* says that loving devotion to God should be pure, singular, and unrivaled by any person, thing, or idea.

2. *You shall not make for yourself an idol* says that loving devotion to God should focus on Him, not on religious practices, props, or substitutes.

3. *You shall not misuse the name of the Lord your God* says that loving devotion to God should include respect and reverence for His person and His name.

4. *Remember the Sabbath day by keeping it holy* says that loving devotion to God should include time spent each week in worship and rest in His honor.

5. *Honor your father and your mother* says that love for parents should be expressed through recognition, respect, and esteem for them.

6. *You shall not murder* says that love for others should be

expressed through high regard for and diligent preservation of human life.

7. *You shall not commit adultery* says that love for spouse (or future spouse) should be demonstrated through sexual purity and faithfulness.

8. *You shall not steal* says that love for others should be expressed through respect for their property and possessions.

9. *You shall not give false testimony* against your neighbor says that love for others should be shown through honesty and truthfulness in all our dealings.

10. *You shall not covet* says that love for others should focus on what we can give to others instead of what we can get that belongs to them.

The numerous other moral principles stated in the Bible—including the instructions of Jesus in the Gospels and of the apostles in the New Testament letters—should be viewed the same way. Each is a specific application of the command to love in a certain setting or relationship. These laws and guidelines define the duty of love in each sphere of responsibility.

God in His wisdom and love spelled out for us the details and implications of the love command in the many moral principles of the Old and New Testaments. The summary is necessary so that we do not forget that love is the heart of each command. But the many laws are necessary so that we have sufficient understanding of the responsibilities of love in given situations. God did not leave us guessing about the meaning or application of love as we relate to Him and people. He spelled it out clearly in the commands "do this" and "don't do that."

The fact that many of the commandments and moral principles in the Bible are negative in form does not mean they are negative in intent. It is much easier to name a few things that are not loving than many things that are. In effect, the commandments are saying that some things are never loving and should be avoided. But everything else can be loving, and it is our obligation to see that our words and actions are loving. Furthermore, the intention behind each negative commandment is positive: Love is the only way to respond and relate to God and others. God was so concerned that we know exactly what it means to love that He spelled it out in His laws. God's law is love put into words.

TOUGH QUESTIONS AND STRAIGHT ANSWERS ABOUT LAW AND LOVE

How should Christians respond to specific Old Testament laws about not eating shellfish or pork or avoiding certain fibers in clothing? How can we know what is cultural and what is universal?

The two aspects of the laws in question are the ceremonial law, governing certain foods and procedures for Old Testament Israel, and the moral law, commandments governing our relationship with God and people. Christians are not under the ceremonial law because Jesus did away with it. He declared all foods ceremonially clean (Mark 7:18–19). Peter heard the message again during his vision at Joppa (Acts 10:15). Paul underscored Christ's declaration in his writing (1 Tim. 4:3–5). But God's moral law is permanent because it reflects His changeless nature (Mal. 3:6; Heb. 6:18; 2 Tim. 2:13). Wherever you find God's moral law showing you how to love Him and love others, it is still in force.

Does the commandment regarding the Sabbath mean that we are sinning if we work or cause someone else to work by eating out or shopping on a Sunday?

Christians today are not under the Old Testament Sabbath law, which is the only one of the Ten Commandments not repeated in the New Testament. If we were under this law, we would have to cease all work between sundown Friday and sundown Saturday, the Jewish Sabbath. However, the moral principle behind the Sabbath law was maintained by the early Christians who reserved the first day of the week—Sunday—for rest and worship (Acts 20:7; 1 Cor. 16:2; Rev. 1:10).

While we are not obligated to keep the Old Testament Sabbath law, nevertheless, we should reserve one day each week for rest and worship (Heb. 10:25). For most of us, Sunday is that day because Christian congregations traditionally meet on Sunday. Those who must work on Sunday, such as emergency service personnel and dairy farmers, should take part of Sunday or another day for worship and rest or seek a rotation schedule in order to attend church on some Sundays. People who elect to work in food service or sales on Sunday should also be careful to take a day off and attend services at other times. We are not necessarily sinning if we eat in a restaurant or buy groceries on Sunday. The responsibility lies with the individuals serving us. If they are intent on obeying God from their hearts, they will choose another day of the week for rest, relaxation, and worship. If they are not so motivated, that is their choice. Whether they serve us or someone else makes no difference.

Is tithing a New Testament practice as well as an Old Testament law? How does tithing demonstrate love to God and others?

Tithing existed long before the law of Moses, having been

practiced by both Abraham (Gen. 14) and Jacob (Gen. 28). And tithing continues into the New Testament. It is mentioned by Jesus in Matthew 23:23 as something worthy of practice and implied by Paul in 1 Corinthians 9:13 and 14 as a means for paying those who minister to us. Tithing seems to be a reasonable minimum standard for Christian giving, with sacrificial offerings added as each individual feels led (2 Cor. 8:3–4). Jesus said, "No one can serve two masters. Either he will hate the one and love the other, or he will be devoted to the one and despise the other. You cannot serve both God and money" (Matt. 6:24). Giving generously and cheerfully reminds us that we serve God, not our money, and demonstrates our love for Him in a tangible way.

The law put love into words so we could understand its meaning. Jesus Christ put love into life so we could fulfill its demands. Jesus said that He came to fulfill the law. He did so by living out the moral principles contained in the Old Testament. Jesus showed us what love for God and people looks like in human behavior, becoming the perfect example for any and all who commit to obey the two greatest commandments.

A LIFE WORTH WATCHING

Human nature is such that a life lived is more impressive to us than a word spoken, especially in the realm of morals and ethics. When it comes to knowing and doing right, there is no substitute for a living example. Jesus Christ was that example for all humanity. His life and ministry on earth personified all the moral precepts contained in the Old Testament. Jesus not only taught the moral law of God, but He also lived it to ultimate perfection. He lived a life truly worth watching.

The most eloquent message preached through the life of Jesus is God's love for His human creation. As John observed, "This is how God showed his love among us: He sent his one and only Son into the world that we might live through him" (1 John 4:9). Christ was God's love gift to us wrapped in human flesh. He was the definitive "word" about God's love in our world (John 1:14). The law of Moses was an expression of God's love in words. The incarnation of Christ was the expression of God's love in human life.

The Bible is very explicit as to the perfection of Christ's life. Peter said, "He committed no sin, and no deceit was found in his mouth" (1 Pet. 2:22). He was "a lamb without blemish or defect" (1:19). Paul declared that Christ "had no sin" (2 Cor. 5:21). He was "tempted in every way, just as we are—yet was without sin" (Heb. 4:15). John's first letter has numerous references to Christ's sinlessness: "In him there is no darkness at all" (1:5); "Jesus Christ, the Righteous One" (2:1); "He is pure" (3:3); "In him is no sin" (3:5). Pilate said, "I find no basis for a charge against this man" (Luke 23:4). Pilate's judgment has been the verdict of history. Jesus lived a truly flawless life.

The perfection of Christ's life was not simply the absence of any wrong; it was the presence of everything right and good, particularly His love. Jesus loved God the Father (John 14:31). He loved His disciples (John 13:1, 17:12, 26). He showed compassion toward the multitudes (Mark 8:2), particularly His own people, the Jews, who rejected Him (Matt. 23:37). He healed the sick, opened the eyes of the blind, raised the dead, and spent

Himself tirelessly in helping others. His life was in fact one continual demonstration of perfect love.

Does it concern you that Jesus' example of love was perfect and yours is often imperfect? Do you sometimes throw up your hands and sigh, "What's the use? I'll never measure up to Christ's example"? Don't be discouraged. Christ is perfect in everything. Even though He encourages us to follow His example (1 Pet. 2:21), He understands our weaknesses and forgives our imperfection. John wrote about this contrast, "I write this to you so that you will not sin. But if anybody does sin, we have one who speaks to the Father in our defense—Jesus Christ, the Righteous One" (1 John 2:1). God's standard is Jesus' perfection (Eph. 4:13); and He is at work in us making us over into the image of His Son (Rom. 8:29; Phil. 2:13). One day, we will be just like Jesus in every respect of character (1 John 3:2). Until then, as we study His example and rely on His strength, we should be more loving this month, this year, this decade than we were the one before. And since He is perfect and we are not, we will always have something to shoot for in the process of learning to love God and people as He loves.

Several important aspects of divine love are dramatically illustrated in Christ's life. A closer look at these areas should encourage your own love to grow.

First, Jesus loved *indiscriminately*. Other Jews avoided the Samaritan woman with the sordid past, but Jesus initiated a conversation that changed her life and the lives of many others (John 4). Jesus spent time with all who sought Him out, even those who were misfits or outcasts. He healed lepers, blind beggars, and raving demoniacs with a word or a touch. He was as much at home with the wealthy as with the poor. He ministered to prostitutes, dishonest tax collectors, Roman soldiers, stuffy

Jewish religious dignitaries, and foreigners. Jesus' example encourages us to look past physical, cultural, and socioeconomic differences to see every individual as someone worthy of our love.

Jesus also loved *unconditionally*. He loved people whether or not they accepted Him as Messiah and Lord. Even though Jesus knew from the beginning that Judas would betray Him (John 13:11), He showed the same concern for the traitor as He did for the other disciples (John 6:70, 71, 17:12). He prayed for those who crucified Him, "Father, forgive them, for they do not know what they are doing" (Luke 23:34). Paul wrote of Christ's unconditional love, "Very rarely will anyone die for a righteous man. . . . But God demonstrates his own love for us in this: While we were still sinners, Christ died for us" (Rom. 5:7–8). Jesus shows us that we must love everyone not because they love us, know us, or care about us at all but because everyone needs God's love, and ours.

Jesus loved *immeasurably*. Paul prayed that we may "grasp how wide and long and high and deep is the love of Christ" (Eph. 3:18). Why do we need to grasp the greatness of Christ's love? Because our love needs to grow wider and longer and higher and deeper to encompass the staggering love needs around us. Christ's love has no end, so we can trust Him to help us develop a love that "always protects, always trusts, always hopes, always perseveres" (1 Cor. 13:7), even for the most unlovable and challenging people.

The essence of Christ's love is that it is *sacrificial*. "God so loved the world that he gave . . ." (John 3:16). The apostle Paul exulted in Christ "who loved me and gave himself for me" (Gal. 2:20). Jesus told His disciples, "Greater love has no one than this, that he lay down his life for his friends" (John 15:13).

Identifying Himself as the good shepherd, He proclaimed, "I lay down my life for the sheep. . . . No one takes it from me, but I lay it down of my own accord" (John 10:15, 18). Sacrificial love is rarely easy or fun. To love people as Christ loved may cost you some time, money, energy, comfort, and convenience. And yet John the apostle of love challenges us, "Jesus Christ laid down his life for us. And we ought to lay down our lives for our brothers" (1 John 3:16). As the grateful recipients of sacrificial love, we must love sacrificially.

Christ's love kept Him *involved* with people. He was not afraid to be in contact with the people who needed His loving words and touch. He attended weddings (John 2); He accepted invitations to banquets from tax collectors and sinners (Matt. 9:9–12); He was even labeled "a friend of tax collectors and 'sinners'" (Matt. 11:19). He mingled with crowds, lived with His disciples, attended holiday feasts, and spent time in the temple and synagogue. Although He occasionally took time out alone for prayer and rest, Jesus was a mixer, pouring Himself into people. To follow His example, we must invest our lives in others even when we would rather not be bothered. This may mean going out with your coworkers after work occasionally in order to build bridges of friendship. It may mean getting involved with your neighbors in a coffee klatch, joining a coed volleyball team at the rec center with your spouse, volunteering for a parent committee at your child's school, or taking a class at the community college. Whenever we get involved with people for the purpose of befriending them, encouraging them, and sharing the good news with them, we are loving as Christ loved.

Christ's love was also *firm*. He was not unloving when He rebuked the Pharisees for their hypocrisy, warning, "Woe to you, teachers of the law and Pharisees, you hypocrites! . . .

Woe to you, blind guides! . . . You snakes! You brood of vipers!" (Matt. 23:13, 16, 33). Nor was He unloving to warn people of the fires of hell (Matt. 5:22; 18:8). As we have discovered, love means to protect and provide for the objects of our love, even if we must lovingly confront them with their sin in hopes of sparing them the painful consequences. Jesus manifested a firmness of love when He expelled the money changers from the temple with a whip (John 2:14–16). Love need not be soft to be kind, for "the Lord disciplines those he loves, and he punishes everyone he accepts as a son" (Heb. 12:6). You are following Christ's example of tough love when you are led to oppose a curriculum in your child's classroom that violates scriptural principles, when you prohibit your children from attending movies you know will negatively affect their morals, or when you question a company policy that is dishonest or unfair. It is less than loving to allow people to turn away from God's ways without a warning simply because we don't want to be unpopular.

A PATTERN WORTH FOLLOWING

The love of Christ, as beautiful as it is, is more than a work of art that we may appreciate and praise. Christ's love is not primarily aesthetic but redemptive and ethical. It is not merely a picture to behold but also a pattern to follow. His love does us little good unless we put it into practice. Jesus is the pattern for the believer's responsibility to love God and people.

The trademark of Christianity is love. Jesus announced, "By this all men will know that you are my disciples, if you love one another" (John 13:35). And He unabashedly pointed to Himself as the pattern for our love of others: "Love each other as I have loved you" (John 15:12). Paul underscored the theme when he wrote, "Live a life of love, just as Christ loved us and gave himself up for us" (Eph. 5:2). Husbands are told, "Love your wives, just as Christ loved the church and gave himself up for her" (Eph. 5:25). It's not enough to appreciate the example; we must follow the pattern.

The Christian's love should be sacrificial just as Christ's love was sacrificial. He laid down His life for us at great personal cost; we must lay down our lives for others even when it costs us something (John 15:13). The Christian's love should be forgiving just as Christ's love was forgiving. As Jesus forgave those who nailed Him to the cross, we must love our enemies and pray for those who persecute us (Matt. 5:44). Stephen's dying prayer for those who stoned him was similar to Jesus' prayer: "Lord, do not hold this sin against them" (Acts 7:60). Paul admonished, "Bless those who persecute you; bless and do not curse. . . . Do not repay anyone evil for evil. . . . If your enemy is hungry, feed him; if he is thirsty, give him something to drink. . . . Do not be overcome by evil, but overcome evil with good" (Rom. 12:14, 17, 20, 21). If you cannot forgive those who wrong you or harm you, you are not loving as Christ loved.

The Christian's love must be firm as Christ's love was firm. Fathers are to love their children, bringing them up "in the training and instruction of the Lord" (Eph. 6:4). In fact, withholding discipline is tantamount to withholding love. Solomon wrote, "He who spares the rod hates his son, but he who loves him is careful to discipline him" (Prov. 13:24). Remember: Love isn't as concerned about giving people what they *want* as about giving them what they *need*. It was firm love that moved Jesus to rebuke Peter: "Get behind me, Satan! You are a stumbling block to me; you do not have in mind the things of God, but the things of men" (Matt. 16:23). And it was firm love that moved the Corinthian Christians to expel an immoral member (1 Cor. 5:5) because "a little yeast works through the whole batch of dough" (v. 6).

Love is forgiving and firm. Love is not naive and sentimental; it is realistic and strong. Following the pattern of Christ's love will equip you to be a person of relevance and influence in your world as well as a channel of comfort and encouragement.

A POWER WORTH RECEIVING

The love of Christ is most eloquently summarized in 1 Corinthians 13, the love chapter. The beauty of Christ's pattern of selfless love is seen when we insert His name for the word *love* in these verses, for God is love and Christ is God's love in human flesh.

If I speak in the tongues of men and of angels, but have not Christ, I am only a resounding gong or a clanging cymbal. If I have the gift of prophecy and can fathom all mysteries and all knowledge, and if I have a faith that can move mountains, but have not Christ, I am nothing. If I give all I possess to the poor and surrender my body to the flames, but have not Christ, I gain nothing.

Christ is patient, Christ is kind. He does not envy, He does not boast, He is not proud. He is not rude, He is not self-seeking, He is not easily angered, He keeps no record of wrongs. Christ does not delight in evil but rejoices with the truth. He always protects, always trusts, always hopes, always perseveres. Christ never fails.

The value of Christ's pattern of love is inestimable. The law spelled out the meaning of love; Christ *lived out* the meaning of love. The law *defined* love; Christ *demonstrated* love. The meaning of love—God's love—could not be more perfectly manifested than in a life of perfect love. Christ's life of love fulfilled what the law required. Paul wrote, "For what the law was powerless to do in that it was weakened by the sinful nature, God did by sending his own Son in the likeness of sinful man to be a sin offering. And so he condemned sin in sinful man, in order that the righteous requirements of the law might be fully met in us, who do not live according to the sinful nature but according to the Spirit" (Rom. 8:3, 4). Christ fulfilled the law *for* us, and He also fulfills the law *in* us. He was the first person to live out the demands of love perfectly, and He will transfer that power to us by the Spirit, for "the fruit of the Spirit is love" (Gal. 5:22).

The value of love lived out in the flesh over love spelled out in the law is quite clear. The law can tell us what love ought to do, but it cannot do it. Christ, however, could. He fulfilled all the demands of the law of love. And by His Spirit, He provides this love for all who are willing to receive it. If you are willing to die to self and allow God's love to flow through you to others, you will receive the power to love as Christ loved. You can say with Paul, "I have been crucified with Christ and I no longer live, but Christ lives in me. The life I live in the body, I live by faith in the Son of God, who loved me and gave himself for me" (Gal. 2:20).

Christ is God's perfect love personified, and Christ lives in you. In order to grasp the significance of God's love operating in and through your life, write your name in the blanks below. Then read these lines from 1 Corinthians 13 aloud to yourself several times.

_____ is patient, _____ is
kind._____does not envy, _____does not
boast, _____is not proud._____ is not rude,
_____is not self-seeking, _____is not easily
angered, _____keeps no record of wrongs.
_____does not delight in evil but rejoices with the
truth. _____always protects, always trusts, always
hopes, always perseveres. _____never fails.

Christ's love is more than a pattern for our lives; it is the very possibility and power enabling us to live a life of perfect love. John said, "Everyone who loves has been born of God and knows God" (1 John 4:7). No one can truly love unless they know God. But if you know God and are filled with His power, the life of love He requires of you is a very achievable possibility.

TOUGH QUESTIONS AND STRAIGHT ANSWERS ABOUT CHRIST'S PATTERN OF LOVE

How can you say that Christ loved the money changers when He overturned their tables and chased them out of the temple with a whip? How does anger fit in with the command to love?

As has already been discussed, sometimes love must be tough. Christ's angry outburst in the temple is an example of tough love in action. His love for the Father would not permit Him to overlook such disrespect for God in the temple. Nor would His love for people allow Him to tolerate their disobedience. His anger was not motivated by hate for the money changers but by love for both God and people. It is similar to how you might react if you were a surgeon and someone came into your operating room without scrubbing up. You would quickly and perhaps sternly chase that person out to protect the patient from germs. Or if you discovered someone robbing the poor or exploiting a widow of her meager income, you would seek to help the victims.

To love doesn't mean that you only do or say what pleases people. Love wills and works for the good of the person loved even when the good may be difficult to receive. You submit your child to the pain of an inoculation or surgery if needed because you love her enough to not see her become ill. You chastise a lazy employee because you love him enough to not let him get fired for his slothfulness. At the core of these difficult actions is your commitment to gain the best for those you love. As Jesus demonstrated, even anger can be an expression of love when the root of that anger is the desire to do what is right for those involved

LOVE IN CONFLICT 12

God is love, and love is of God. So in God there is no conflict of love. There is perfect harmony among God the Father—the great Lover—His beloved Son, and the Spirit of love. But on earth it's a different story. The various duties of love sometimes conflict even for those who are most determined to love as Christ loved. Responsibilities of love overlap and duties clash, bringing tension. Sometimes two or more commandments conflict. How do we decide between them? Sometimes none of the options open to us seems the loving thing to do. Where do we go for answers? These dilemmas put our love commitment to the test.

God's people in the Bible have often faced ethical dilemmas in which the loving choice was difficult to discern. For example:

- It is wrong for the patriarch Abraham to kill his son, and it is wrong for him to dis-

LOVE IS ALWAYS RIGHT

obey God. How does he decide what to do when God
instructs him to offer Isaac as a human sacrifice? (See
Genesis 22.)

- God commands obedience to the Pharaoh of Egypt, but
the Pharaoh commands the murder of Israel's innocent
boy babies. How do the midwives decide what to do?
(See Exodus 1.)

- The Bible forbids lying, but Israel's spies will be killed if
Rahab reveals their hiding place to inquiring soldiers.
What should she do? (See Joshua 2.)

- The queen commands that all God's prophets be killed.
But Obadiah defies her and hides one hundred of them.
Is Obadiah doing the loving thing? (See 1 Kings 18.)

- Abraham fears for the safety of his wife, so he tells the
king that she is his sister. Is Abraham's lie the loving
thing to do? (See Genesis 20.)

- Murder is forbidden by God. But King Saul is mortally
wounded and orders his armor-bearer to put him out of
his misery. Is the servant right to kill his king? (See 1
Samuel 31.)

These situations may seem distant and detached from contemporary experiences. After all, sacrifices, warring monarchies,
and rather primitive customs are not part of our culture. But we
face our own share of love conflicts that are no less ambiguous
and challenging. For example, how do you decide the loving
thing to do when:

- the commandments say you shall not kill but your government sends you into battle to exercise lethal force in
defense of democracy?

154

- as a Christian teen, your parents forbid you from serving God or talking with other Christians?

- your wife suffers severe complications during delivery and is near death, and you must choose between trying to save her life or saving the life of your baby?

- a fellow employee makes you vow secrecy then confesses that she is extorting money from your company?

- your ninety-year-old grandfather, suffering continual, excruciating pain from a terminal illness, begs you to hand him enough pills to "take me into the arms of Jesus and sweet peace"?

- a drug-crazed individual enters the restaurant where you are eating with your parents, spouse, and children and begins shooting wildly, and you can either kill him or throw yourself into the line of fire to save others?

These examples only scratch the surface of a plethora of ethical dilemmas that test our understanding of and commitment to love. In many situations like these, the most loving choice is not always obvious. How do we decide what to do?

DEAD-END PATHS TO RESOLVING LOVE IN CONFLICT

There are believers who have suggested several different ways to face the issue of love in conflict. The following responses may appear to offer a clear path to a biblical solution, but they prove to be dead ends in the effort to exercise love in real life.

There is only one absolute duty of love, therefore there is no conflict. This line of thought contends that it takes two absolutes to have an absolute conflict. But since there is only one absolute duty of love, then all conflicts are apparent but not real. In every situation there is only one absolute duty: Do the most loving thing possible.

This is a simple, straightforward approach free of the baggage of numerous ethical commandments that often seem in conflict with each other. It also preserves the absolute nature of love and calls the believer to simply make the most godlike or loving response. And it is broadly applicable. The general rule is to love, but the particular meaning of love will be determined by the specific situation.

But this approach falls short of being helpful in ethical dilemmas. First, there is not just one absolute duty of love. There are at least two: love God and love people. As Abraham discovered when caught between God and his son Isaac, these two sometimes come into conflict. And it won't do to say that loving God is an absolute and loving people is not. Both are commanded by God.

Furthermore, the one-absolute ethic is too general to be meaningful. Telling us to do the most loving thing possible without spelling out how we can determine what it is leaves us in a quandary. Without the commandments and Christ's example Christians would not know what the absolute obligations of love really are, to say nothing of being able to perform them. We are left to our own subjective intuitions and guesses.

Another dead-end line of thought states: *Moral conflicts are false dilemmas because God always provides a way out, a third option.* Christians who take this tack assert that God is faithful to those who are faithful to His law, and He will in a seeming conflict always "provide a way out so that you can stand up under it" (1 Cor. 10:13). God intervened and saved Abraham from having to kill Isaac, and He will do the same for anyone else who is faithful to His commands.

These people cite incidents like the following from World War II to prove that God provides a way out of moral dilemmas when people have committed to obey His commandments. German soldiers burst into a home of Jewish sympathizers where Jews were secreted under the floorboards. "Are you hiding Jews in this home?" the soldiers demanded. A child who had been taught never to lie innocently blurted out, "Yes sir, they are under the kitchen table." But instead of checking for a trapdoor, the soldiers laughed and said, "That's ridiculous. There is obviously no one under the table." They left and the Jews were miraculously spared even though their location had been revealed. "God provided a way out for the Jews and their hosts when the truth was told," some say, "and He will do the same for us."

This view is at first commendable because it maintains without compromise that there are many absolute commands of love in Scripture, not just one virtually meaningless and irrelevant norm. The assumption is that, if God issued both supposedly conflicting commands, He expects us to keep both, and He will see to it that we can do so without sinning.

But are all moral conflicts merely apparent and not real? Is there always a third way out of every dilemma? The evidence is to the contrary. Abraham did not have to kill his son, but *he intended to do so*, and Jesus taught that morality is a matter of intent (Matt. 5:21, 22, 27, 28). The Hebrew midwives saved children's lives, but they had to disobey the government to do so. Moses' parents hid their infant son instead of handing him over to the Pharaoh's executioner as commanded. They were not scolded by God for their disobedience but praised for their faith (Heb. 11:23).

Furthermore, this view assumes that all commandments are of equal force. But they are not. Love for God is the "first and greatest commandment" (Matt. 22:38). The second commandment, love for others, is *like* the first but not *equal* to it (v. 39). There are occasions when love for God is in conflict with love for people, and on those occasions, love for God comes first. If and when God miraculously provides a way to accommodate both, we are thankful. But history reveals that God does not always respond this way. God's people have often had to choose to obey God *rather* than people—and God honored those choices.

Another fruitless way of thinking declares: *When we cannot avoid breaking one commandment to obey another, we must simply choose the lesser of the two evils.* This view urges us to always choose the least nonloving option available in the face of a moral conflict. Of course, when we break one of God's commandments under any circumstances, we are guilty of sin. The providence of God does not always supply a way to escape sinning, but thankfully the love of God provides forgiveness for those who confess. So the apostles obviously had to confess their sin of disobeying the Jewish rulers in order to obey God's mandate to preach. And the young person who must choose between obeying God and obeying his parents must obey God and at the same time seek and receive God's forgiveness for violating the fifth commandment.

This approach has some major problems. First, would an all-wise, all-loving God judge someone guilty for doing what was unavoidable? If our best choice is the lesser of two evils, is it right for God to blame us for doing the best we could do? Hardly. It seems inconsistent with the nature of God as revealed in Scripture to set up absolute but conflicting commands and then pronounce us guilty for choosing one of them, even if it is the best choice. A person is guilty only if the action is avoidable.

Second, if even the right choice in a moral conflict is sin, what does that say about the sinlessness of Christ? For example, Jesus affirmed the commandment to honor father and mother (Matt. 15:4, 19:19). But on at least one occasion, Jesus kept His mother waiting to see Him because He was busy serving other people (Matt. 12:46–49). And in order to obey the Father and offer His life as the sacrifice for sin, Jesus had to leave His mother in the care of others (John 19:25–27). In situations like these and perhaps many others, Jesus disobeyed the lesser of two or more conflicting commandments. In so doing, He was either guilty of sin—which the Scriptures soundly refute (Heb. 4:15)—or there are no situations where a lesser good is called for. There is always a positive good possible in every moral choice, and choosing the greater good transcends any duty to the lesser good.

Third, since God calls us to obedience and holiness, why would He put us in a situation where every choice is wrong? It makes no sense to say we are morally obligated to do the lesser evil. This would mean it is right to do wrong, it is okay to sin, which is unbiblical.

ALWAYS OPT FOR THE GREATER GOOD

Love is never caught on the horns of a dilemma. There are levels and spheres of love, and one is always higher than another. Each love command is absolute *in its* area. But when that area overlaps with another area, then the lower responsibility of love should be subordinated to the higher. For example, when the two conflict, duty to God has priority over duty to people, which Abraham demonstrated with his son Isaac. The Hebrew midwives obeyed the greater obligation to save human lives over the lesser one of telling the truth to the king who sought to kill the babies.

Each of the absolute commandments of the Bible is binding on the relationship it specifies. Adultery is always wrong as such. Murder is never right in itself. Lying is universally wrong as such. However, when one or more of these relationships, which are wrong in themselves, overlaps with another, our duty to the lower may be suspended in view of our responsibility to the higher. For example, if you awake to find a knife-wielding burglar in your bedroom, the prohibition against killing is suspended in favor of the obligation to protect your spouse and children. There are no *exceptions* to absolute commands, but there are some *exemptions* in view of higher priorities of love. There is always a greater good.

Furthermore, because God has given us many laws defining the nature and areas of love, we can know in advance what to do in a given situation. This places the Christian love ethic in direct opposition to situation ethics. Situation ethics claims that the situation determines the loving thing to do. God's love ethic prescribes in advance what must be done in every situation even when commandments conflict. We must always opt for the greater good.

The fact that there are greater and lesser goods is clear in Scripture. Jesus spoke of "more important matters of the law" (Matt. 23:23). Justice and mercy have greater weight than tithing on the scale of God's values although the law required both (Matt. 23:23). Helping someone in need, such as the work of feeding the hungry or healing the sick, was more important to Jesus than not keeping the Sabbath (Matt. 12:1–5).

The two great commands of Jesus reveal greater and lesser goods. Love for God is a greater good than love for people

(Matt. 10:37). Your love for God may lead you to disobey the government if it commands you to sin, but love for country should never lead you to disobey God under any circumstances. Love for family is a greater good than love for strangers (1 Tim. 5:8). Providing for believers is a greater good than providing for unbelievers (Gal. 6:10). A more detailed hierarchy of greater and lesser goods suggested in Scripture will be discussed in the next chapter.

The whole concept of rewards is built on the premise that some activities are better than others. In Jesus' parable of the ten servants, one who did very well was given charge of ten cities; one who didn't do as well received five cities (Luke 19:12–26). Paul wrote to believers, "We must all appear before the judgment seat of Christ, that each one may receive what is due him for the things done while in the body, whether good or bad" (2 Cor. 5:10). Some people will receive a crown and some will not (Rev. 3:11). The works of some will prove to be "gold, silver, and costly stones" while others will be likened to "wood, hay, or straw" (1 Cor. 3:12). Each day we are presented with opportunities in which we may choose greater or lesser goods for which we will receive greater or lesser rewards.

Just as there are greater and lesser goods there are greater and lesser evils. All sins are sin, but not all sins are equally sinful. James wrote, "Whoever keeps the whole law and yet stumbles at just one point is guilty of breaking all of it" (James 2:10). He was speaking of unity of the law, not equality of sin. James recognized greater and lesser goods when he suggested that teachers of the Word are more responsible than those who are not teachers (James 3:1). Jesus indicated that thinking adulterous thoughts are also sinful, just as committing an adulterous act. But the act is a greater evil than the thought because the act will negatively impact more people than will the thought.

So there are degrees of good and degrees of evil. Some acts are better and some worse than others. Indeed, Jesus spoke of "a greater sin" (John 19:11). Good and evil are ranked in a pyramid with the best at the top, the worst on the bottom, and varying degrees of good and evil in between. Some single immoral acts are more vicious than numerous other acts of evil. For example, one brutal act of murder can be more evil than many little white lies. Therefore, whenever we are faced with a conflict between good alternatives or between good and evil, the morally right course of action is always the greatest good or the most loving response. In fact, opting for something less than the greatest good can be evil. For example, if a man rescues two people from drowning but could just as easily have rescued five, his good is marred by sin. James declared, "Anyone, then, who knows the good he ought to do and doesn't do it, sins" (4:17).

Therefore, since moral acts have different values, it is necessary for Christians to weigh the alternatives for love in order to choose the greatest good or the most loving response. This is often a difficult task, but it is not impossible when we know the divine scale of values from Scripture.

The basis for determining greater and lesser goods is the greatest of all goods, God. But since we cannot ask God directly, we must find absolute goodness in His law and His Son, which are presented to us in the Bible. The Word of God is the criterion for measuring greater and lesser goods. The value of an act, then, is determined by how Christlike or godlike it is. And ethical priorities are determined by how near or far they are from absolute love as found in God's law and Christ's life. The more Christlike the act, the greater the good; the closer the resemblance to God's perfect love, the more loving it is.

This points out a major difference between the absolute ethic of love and many other contemporary ethics. The Christian ethic is determined by revealed *rules* not by anticipated *results*. In many circles it is common to determine what is ethically right by estimating what will bring the greatest good to the greatest number of people in the long run. This view, called utilitarianism, was originated by philosopher Jeremy Bentham and advanced by John Stuart Mill in the early nineteenth century. It sounds good, but the differences between the utilitarian approach and the Christian approach to determining good are crucial.

First, utilitarians focus on the desired results and plan their response accordingly. Christians focus on the most loving response as revealed in the rules and principles of Scripture and leave the long-range results to God. We do not determine the rule by the results; the best possible results will occur when we keep the rule God has already established.

Second, God's rules for determining the greater good are absolute; utilitarian rules are generalizations based on past experiences that achieved the greatest results. Christian ethical principles are rooted in the nature and will of God, so they are universally applicable and absolutely binding. Utilitarian rules are subject to unspecified exceptions that will justify the results.

Third, for utilitarians, an action is good only if it brings good consequences. For Christians, an action is good simply if it complies with God's commands apart from the consequences. For example, if a man fails in his best attempt to rescue a drowning person, utilitarians would say it was not a good act because it failed. For Christians, the loving attempt is good whether or not it results in a rescue.

Christians enjoy several advantages over utilitarians. We do not determine what is right and wrong; God has already decided it and revealed it in His Word. We decide only which thought or action will be in accord with what God has revealed to be right. Further, we don't have to figure out the loving thing to do in a conflict situation. God has already revealed His loving priorities in Scripture. Finally, we don't have to guess long-range results based on human experience to determine the best course of action. We simply take the course of action God has revealed and allow Him to take care of the long-range results.

DOING OUR PART

The Christian love ethic is not a software program that spits out answers to love conflicts without struggle or decisions on our part. Rather, it takes real dedication and effort to consistently choose the greatest good and most loving response. We must fill our minds and hearts with the Scriptures in order to know God's nature of love, His laws, and the exemplary life of His Son. Jesus charged the religious people of His day, "You are in error because you do not know the Scriptures or the power of God" (Matt. 22:29). The more you internalize God's Word, the better prepared you will be to discern right choices in conflict situations.

Furthermore, we must be directly involved in prayerfully weighing the alternatives to discover the course of action most in accord with scriptural commands. This is not a task you can pawn off on your parents, Bible study leader, or pastor. It's your decision, so you must consider the options and seek God's guidance in Scripture and prayer yourself. Then you must act on what you decide. Merely knowing the right thing to do is not sufficient; you must take the necessary steps to transform ethic into action.

What is the Holy Spirit's role in this process? It is the Holy Spirit who reveals truth to us and enables us to take action on it (John 16:13). Without Spirit-revealed principles for action and Spirit-empowered motivation to perform what is right, there can be no Christian ethic. We know that the Spirit of God will not lead us apart from or in conflict with the Word of God. The truth God reveals by His Spirit is the truth contained in the Scriptures. The Bible is sufficient for faith and practice; it is a complete revelation of God's absolute love (2 Tim. 3:16–17). There are no moral situations we face for which there are no principles in God's Word. The Holy Spirit's role is to illuminate God's truth to us so we can make the right decisions. He does this by reminding us of a principle in the Bible we may have forgotten, directing us to a principle we haven't yet discovered, or giving us new insight into principles we are already using.

But in all these cases, the Holy Spirit directs us into the Bible for the answer. In no case should we ever seek to go beyond or around what is written in God's Word. It is God's way of helping us discern and do the greatest, most loving good even in the most difficult situations.

TOUGH QUESTIONS AND STRAIGHT ANSWERS ABOUT LOVE IN CONFLICT

What about the miraculous power of God? Can't we expect God to intervene in situations when love is in conflict?

God is all powerful and all loving, but He is not our personal genie in a bottle waiting to bail us out of every problem or moral dilemma. We are promised God's presence with us always (Matt. 28:20), but nowhere in Scripture are we promised that God will always intervene and save us from moral conflicts. Shadrach, Meshach, and Abednego understood this, stating to King Nebuchadnezzar, "If we are thrown into the blazing furnace, the God we serve is able to save us from it, and he will rescue us from your hand, O king. But *even if he does not*, we want you to know, O king, that we will not serve your gods or worship the image of gold you have set up" (Dan. 3:17–18; emphasis added).

Expecting a miracle in every tight squeeze shifts the responsibility for right choices and actions from us to God, something He does not intend. It is a mentality that suggests, "Whenever you're in trouble, punt to God." We have His Word to direct us and His Spirit to encourage and comfort us. These are miracles in themselves, and they are available to us at all times. We should never base a present decision on the possibility that God may perform a spectacular miracle in the future. This is tantamount to putting God to the test, something we are never to do (Matt. 4:7). Rather we are to utilize the resources He has already given and trust His presence as we work through life's difficulties and dilemmas.

VALUE PRINCIPLES FOR RESOLVING LOVE IN CONFLICT

13

W hen the various levels of love overlap or conflict, God's Word calls us to follow the higher love obligation. Behind each of the conflicting situations is one or more scriptural principles indicating which is the greater good. These principles emerge as the light of God's unchanging love passes through the prism of human experience, casting a spectrum or order of God's values. We will consider a number of general value principles in this chapter and a more specialized category of values in the following chapter.

DO IT GOD'S WAY OR MY WAY?

Are any of the following scenarios familiar to you?

The alarm sounds, launching you into a familiar predawn struggle. You know you should get up and keep your daily appointment with God. Your day always goes better after a time of Bible reading and prayer. And if you don't do it early, your busy schedule won't let you get to it later. But you had a late committee meeting at church last night and you're really tired. You want to give yourself a break and sleep through devotions.

◆

Your little nest egg has been growing for months, and you finally have enough money for the new entertainment center you want. But your pastor just announced a big fund-raising campaign for a new building. He has called on the congregation to consider making a financial sacrifice so that others may be reached for Christ. You feel led to put a certain amount into the fund, but to do so you will have to delay the purchase of your new toy.

◆

You have planned a quiet Friday evening at home after a very hectic week. You're looking forward to curling up with a good book or video and not talking to anyone. The phone rings, but you pretend not to be home and listen in as the caller leaves a message on the machine. It's an acquaintance of yours from church who is distraught over a relationship problem. She wants to talk to you as soon as you "get in." You are moved by the caller's problem and think you should pick up the phone and help her. But you also hate to give away the Friday night you have been saving for yourself.

How do you respond in such situations? A primary and often repeated conflict in our lives arises between love for God and love for self. Your commitment to love and serve God may be strong, and your commitment to nourish and cherish yourself for all the right reasons may be healthy. But as the examples above illustrate, they occasionally clash. And when they do, the greater good is to love God above self. Jesus said, "If anyone comes to me and does not hate his father and mother, his wife and children, his brothers and sisters—*yes, even his own life*—he cannot be my disciple" (Luke 14:26; emphasis added). Jesus also modeled this value principle. He prayed in the garden, "My Father, if it is possible, may this cup be taken from me. Yet not as I will, but as you will" (Matt. 26:39). Jesus was fully man as well as fully God. In His humanity, He would have avoided the painful, humiliating death that awaited Him. But His love for the Father superseded even His desire for self-preservation.

Joseph faced another expression of the conflict between love for God and self when Potiphar's wife tried to seduce him. Joseph had much to gain by yielding to the temptation: the favor of his master's wife, possible continued promotion as their household servant, and the fulfillment of normal sexual drives. But Joseph responded, "How then could I do such a wicked thing and sin against God?" (Gen. 39:9). He would not elevate his needs and pleasures above his love for God.

Moses had the choice to remain a pampered prince in Egypt or obey God's call to become Israel's deliverer. Moses opted for the greater good, choosing "to be mistreated along with the people of God rather than to enjoy the pleasures of sin for a short time" (Heb. 11:25).

Paul exhorted believers, "Offer your bodies as living sacrifices, holy and pleasing to God—this is your spiritual act of worship" (Rom. 12:1). Does this mean that God wants us to burn up all our time, energy, and resources serving Him and others, leaving nothing for ourselves? No. Scripture also admonishes us to diligently care for ourselves so we are able to care for others. However, everything we are and have belongs to God. He knows our needs for rest, recreation, growth, and health. He wants us to be mentally, physically, spiritually, and socially healthy. But when His plans conflict with our plans, we must say yes to Him, as in the following examples:

If you're tempted to turn off the alarm and sleep through your personal time with God, choose the greater good. Get up and have devotions. If lack of sleep is a continuing problem, either get to bed earlier, take a catnap in the afternoon, or reschedule your devotions for later in the day.

If you're convinced that God is calling you to postpone buying a new toy and instead direct the money into ministry, choose the greater good. God isn't against entertainment centers as such, but your obedience demonstrates that you love Him supremely.

When an obviously God-ordained ministry opportunity interrupts your schedule, choose the greater good. That may mean setting aside your plans in order to meet the need, or it may mean setting up an appointment with an individual, thus preserving your needed alone time while still making yourself available to serve.

There is an underlying scriptural value principle that governs the area of love for God versus love for people: *God, the Infinite person, is more worthy of love than finite self.* In a conflict between the two, the latter must be subordinated to the former.

YIELD TO GOD OR TO HUMAN AUTHORITY?

Charlene's boss Rene hurried into the office. "When central accounting calls about our monthly report," she said, "tell them it's in the mail."

"But the report isn't even finished, is it?" Charlene asked.

"No, but Danielson doesn't need to know that," Rene said. "As long as he thinks it's on the way, he'll get off my back."

"I can't do that, Rene," Charlene answered. "I know you're under a lot of pressure from Danielson, but I can't lie about the report."

"You're not telling the lie, Charlene, I am," Rene argued, a little put off. "You're just delivering the message."

"I'm sorry, Rene. I can't do it and I won't do it. It's not right."

Rene stared coldly at her assistant. "Do you realize that your lack of cooperation here could have a negative effect on your performance review?"

Charlene dropped her head. "I'm sorry to hear that, but I still can't lie for you. It's against everything I stand for as a Christian."

Rene turned and stormed out of the office without another word.

Love has two basic levels: the vertical responsibility to love God with all our heart and soul and the horizontal responsibility to love our neighbors as ourselves. In the event of a conflict between loving God and loving people, love for God must come first. Jesus illustrated this principle by referring to levels of human love very close to everyone: "Anyone who loves his father or mother more than me is not worthy of me; anyone who loves his son or daughter more than me is not worthy of me" (Matt. 10:37). Our love for God is to be so strong that our love for others, even dear family members, may seem like hate by comparison (Luke 14:26). This does not mean God gives us license to hate others. We are to love people as fully as we love ourselves. But even intense love for parents and children should pale in comparison to our supreme love for God.

The Bible abounds with examples of people who faced conflict between the vertical and horizontal dimensions of love and chose the greater good. Abraham loved God more than he loved his son, Isaac, raising the knife to sacrifice the boy before God finally intervened (Gen. 22). The Hebrew midwives loved God more than they feared the king, sparing the lives of babies in disobedience to the king's command (Exod. 1). Daniel loved God more than he revered King Darius, refusing to give up his daily prayers (Dan. 6). The magi loved God more than they honored jealous King Herod, remaining silent about the identity and location of the Christ child (Matt. 2). The apostles loved God more than they esteemed the religious authorities, refusing to keep silent when commanded not to preach (Acts 4).

Choosing God over people—particularly human authorities— is not always easy. Many people in the Bible whose love for God clashed with the ungodly demands of earthly authorities faced unpleasant repercussions. Some were miraculously delivered, but others were not. Regarding Christians who refused when ordered to renounce their faith in Christ, the writer of Hebrews reported, "Some faced jeers and flogging, while still others were chained and put in prison. They were stoned; they were sawed in two; they were put to death by the sword. They went about in sheepskins and goatskins, destitute, persecuted and mistreated" (11:36, 37). God does not guarantee a life free of trouble for those who seek to obey the great commandment, but He does promise to stay with us through any consequences we may face from putting Him first (Matt. 28:20).

The value principle at work here is based on God's laws and Christ's example: *God, the infinite person, is more worthy of love than finite persons.* Love for God and love for people usually will not conflict in our lives. But when they do, the highest expression of love possible is to honor and obey God no matter what the cost. For example, if a Christian wife is told by her husband to "forget all about God and that Christianity stuff," the greater good is to love God and disregard her husband's demand, even if her stand leads to separation. A child's honor for his parents must end at the point where the parent says, "I forbid you from being a Christian." When a young woman's boyfriend pressures her with, "If you love me, you'll go to bed with me," her love obligation to love God is higher, even if her boyfriend consequently leaves her. And the Christian worker who loves God supremely cannot obey an employer who orders him to dishonestly juggle figures or lie.

TELL THE TRUTH OR PROTECT A LIFE?

A cousin who has been under a doctor's care for clinical depression comes to live with you during her recovery. You were warned that she has tendencies toward suicide and once threatened to overdose on prescription drugs. One night she says, "I need something to put me to sleep. Do you have any sleeping pills in the house?" Immediately you remember a nearly full bottle of potent pills buried in the medicine cabinet. An overdose could be lethal. Fearing that your cousin may go looking for the pills later if you tell her the truth, you answer with a straight face, "No, we never keep old prescription drugs in the house. We always destroy them."

Not all conflicts involve a clear-cut choice between loving God or people. Sometimes the choice is between two spheres where human love operates, as the paragraph above illustrates. Does love for your cousin demand that you reveal the whereabouts of lethal drugs or that you purposely lie to protect her from the temptation to suicide? Is telling a lie to save a human life a loving thing to do? Is it right to tell a lie to protect innocent or defenseless people? You leave your teenage daughter home alone for the evening. You instruct her, "If a stranger phones, don't say we're out. Say, 'My parents are busy at the moment. Can they call you back?'" Is it wrong to instruct your child to purposely deceive others in hopes of protecting her from the possibility of an evil person looking for girls home alone?

The answer depends on how we define *lie*. Are we morally obligated to speak and act truthfully under all circumstances? The ninth commandment states, "You shall not give false testimony against your neighbor" (Exod. 20:16). Proverbs 14:25 reads, "A truthful witness saves lives, but a false witness is deceitful." Ananias and Sapphira were struck dead on the spot for lying to the Holy Spirit (Acts 5). But Rahab lied to the soldiers searching for Israel's spies (Josh. 2). The Hebrew midwives lied to the king, claiming that they could not kill the Hebrew babies because they were born and hidden away before they arrived (Exod. 1). If lying is wrong, why were these people not judged for their transgressions?

Consider the Hebrew midwives. The Scriptures inform us that because they protected innocent lives, "God was kind to the midwives and the people increased and became even more numerous. And because the midwives feared God, he gave them families of their own" (Exod. 1:20, 21). It is hard to believe that their lie was not an essential part of their love for the newborn children they spared and for God. Again, they chose the greater good even though lying in itself is always sinful.

Take Rahab as another example. Although lying is a sin, Rahab chose the greater good of protecting the spies. There are several reasons for believing that Rahab's lie may have been the best thing to do in this conflict situation. First, the Scriptures nowhere condemn her explicitly. Second, Joshua commanded that she and her household be spared when Jericho was attacked "because she hid the spies we sent" (Josh. 6:17). Her lie was the essential element in hiding the spies. So in effect she was to be preserved from the judgment of God on Jericho because she saved the spies' lives. Third, Rahab hid the spies because of her faith in God (Josh. 2:9–13). Hebrews 11:31 records, "By faith the prostitute Rahab, because she welcomed the spies, was not killed with those who were disobedient." Therefore, it appears that her lie was actually an expression of her faith in God. James wrote, "Was not even Rahab the prostitute considered righteous for what she did when she gave lodging to the spies and sent them off in a different direction?" (2:25). It is apparent that Rahab's lie enabled her to express her faith in God. She was commended and not judged for what she did.

Immanuel Kant was so committed to the truth that he claimed he would refuse to intentionally deceive a criminal in order to save the life of the criminal's would-be victim. Despite biblical examples to the contrary, many Christians follow Kant. In so doing, they are saying that the duty to tell the truth to the guilty is a greater good than the duty to save the life of the innocent. And yet many of these people leave the lights on in their homes while they are away to make would-be burglars think they are home. Surely it is not right to deceive in order to save a TV, a stereo, or jewelry but wrong to deceive to save a human life! What would these people do if a madman with a gun demanded to know where their loved ones were? Would they say, "I cannot tell a lie. My family is defenseless and hiding in the closet"? Furthermore, should military leaders, scientists, and intelligence personnel give away the secrets of national security because someone asks? Surely the right of the innocent to live has priority over the right of the guilty to have correct information.

Lying is always wrong as such and never justifiable or right in itself. We are exempt from obedience to the law against lying only when it is preempted by a greater obligation. When telling the truth endangers innocent lives, the greater good is to preserve innocent lives. It is important to note that lying in this context is not an *exception* to the law but merely a temporary *exemption* based on the scriptural priority of a greater good.

The value principle involved is this: *Innocent persons are more worthy of loving respect than persons who promote nonloving activity.* When there is no way to respect the demands of both, innocent lives must take precedence over information that would give advantage to those who would unjustly hurt or kill.

LOVE PEOPLE AND USE THINGS

Few value principles receive more emphasis in Scripture than this one: *People are to be loved over things.* Things not only refers to inanimate objects and animals but also to impersonal activities and rituals, even religious activities. When love for God and people comes into conflict with material possessions or activities, people are always more important than things.

The person of God, of course, is more valuable than anything and all things in the world. Jesus instructed, "Do not store up for yourselves treasures on earth, where moth and rust destroy, and where thieves break in and steal. . . . You cannot serve both God and money. . . . But seek first his kingdom and his righteousness, and all these things [basic material needs] will be given to you as well" (Matt. 6:19, 24, 33). God is to be valued even above the necessities of life.

People created in God's image are also more valuable than things. Jesus said, "What good is it for a man to gain the whole world, yet forfeit his soul?" (Mark 8:36). Nothing in this world, not even sacred things, is as valuable as a human life. Jesus affirmed the action of David, who with his soldiers entered the temple and ate the consecrated bread, which was forbidden (Matt. 12:3, 4). The men were hungry, and they were more important than a law keeping them from satisfying their hunger. The four men who broke a hole in the roof to bring a sick friend to Jesus apparently valued life over things, and Jesus commended their faith (Mark 2:1–5).

Jesus demonstrated that one human life was more important than animals when he cast the demons out of a man and into a herd of pigs (Mark 5:11–13). He at least implied that people are more valuable than money, even tithes, when He said, "You give a tenth of your spices—mint, dill and cumin. But you have neglected the more important matters of the law—justice, mercy and faithfulness. You should have practiced the latter, without neglecting the former" (Matt. 23:23). Paul stated, "The love of money is a root of all kinds of evil" (1 Tim. 6:10). Things are not to be loved more than people. Things are not even to be loved; they are to be used in loving God and people.

Does this mean we are not to have or desire things? Are all Christians subject to Jesus' instruction to the rich young man: "Go, sell your possessions and give to the poor, and you will have treasure in heaven. Then come, follow me" (Matt. 19:21)? Is it wrong to be financially sound or even wealthy? No, the Bible does not condemn possessions or wealth as such. There were many wealthy people in Scripture who loved God: Abraham,

David, Solomon, Joseph of Arimathea, Lydia. Rather the Bible speaks against preoccupation with money or material possessions. First Timothy 6:10 is often misquoted as "Money is the root of all evil." It actually reads, "The *love of money* is a root of all kinds of evil," adding "Some people, eager for money, have wandered from the faith and pierced themselves with many griefs."

It is not necessarily wrong to earn a lot of money, have a large bank account, and own nice things. But if our money or possessions block us from loving God and people, the greater good is to give up things in deference to the needs of people. John charged, "If anyone has material possessions and sees his brother in need but has no pity on him, how can the love of God be in him?" (1 John 3:17). To love God and people first means to keep a loose grip on money and things and generously share both in loving service of others.

A correlative principle to loving persons over things is: An unborn person is more valuable than any thing. An unborn child is worth more than a fully grown, million-dollar race horse. An unborn child is worth more than the world's largest diamond. An unborn child is worth more than a career, a fancy car, or a vacation home. An unborn human being is not mere tissue or an appendage of the body. It is a person created in the image of God. Those who tamper with an emerging human life cradled in a mother's womb are interrupting the work of God (Ps. 139:14–16). No amount of money or earthly goods are worth the sacrifice of a developing human being. In fact, capital punishment was the sentence in the Old Testament for causing a premature birth that resulted in the death of the child (Exod. 21:22–23).

SACRIFICING A FEW FOR THE SAKE OF MANY

We have seen it in the movies and heard about it in real accounts of war. A live hand grenade lands in the center of a platoon of soldiers. While his comrades cower in fear, one self-less, brave soldier dives on the grenade to smother a lethal blast that could have killed several. One person sacrifices his life to save many. The scene illustrates a rather obvious guideline for love in conflict: *All other things being equal, love demands that many lives are more important than a few lives.* Samson sacrificed his own life to take the lives of the enemy and thus save his people (Judg. 16:29, 30). David killed Goliath to protect the many lives of his countrymen (1 Sam. 17). Caiaphas, the high priest at the time of Jesus' crucifixion, used this principle when counseling the Jews that "it would be good if one man died for the people" (John 18:14). It was an unwitting prediction of Christ's atoning sacrifice for all the world (Rom. 5:15). The apostle Paul said he was willing to exchange his eternal soul for the salvation of his people, the Jews (Rom. 9:3).

Scripture supports the principle that many are more valuable than few. God told Adam, "Be fruitful and increase in number; fill the earth and subdue it" (Gen. 1:28), and He repeated the command to Noah after the flood (Gen. 9:1). However, the word *fill* suggests limits to the principle, that is, many are better than few but not better than too many. Furthermore, God offers salvation to all, not just a few—"not wanting anyone to perish, but everyone to come to repentance" (2 Pet. 3:9).

Practically speaking, we cannot love everyone, so we must love as many as possible. We must try to reach as many of our family members, neighbors, and coworkers for Christ as we can. We must support as many Christian ministries as possible with our giving and praying. And if we must choose, we ought to support ministries that are doing the most good for the most people.

Implied in the illustrations so far is that *all other things are equal*. Does the principle change when things are not equal? Yes. The Bible contains numerous examples of a few righteous taking priority over *many* wicked. Why, if all lives have equal value intrinsically? Because sometimes the few are the key to saving the many. Righteous Noah and his family were preserved while the rest of the population of the wicked world perished (1 Pet. 3:20). God destroyed the many wicked of Sodom and saved only the few righteous of Lot's family (Gen. 19). The Israelites were commanded to exterminate all the wicked Canaanite nations (Lev. 18:24–25). But in all these cases, the few were the key to saving the many.

We must certainly love the lost and seek to turn them toward Christ. But we must invest quality time in nourishing and cherishing the family of God with whom we will spend eternity. Spending time discipling five believers who may each in turn reach five unbelievers is better than trying to convert five resistant unbelievers, though each activity is important. We must love and reach out to the most we can with preference given to our family and the family of God.

THE LIVES OF THE MOTHER AND HER UNBORN CHILD

In a society that is hotly divided on the issue of abortion, another biblical value principle must be presented. It has been stated that an unborn person is more valuable than any material things. However, *the life of an unborn child must be preserved at all costs except when the life of the mother is in jeopardy*. If a mother's life is threatened by a tubal pregnancy, the unborn fetus must be removed to save the mother. Furthermore, if a man must choose between saving the life of his wife or a near-term fetus, the mother should be saved at the sacrifice of the fetus. But if the choice is between a mother dying of cancer and the healthy fetus she carries, the principle is no longer definitive. Similarly, if a choice must be made between an infant and an advanced Alzheimer's patient or a living "vegetable," the value principle that follows comes into play.

Usually there is not a conflict in these areas. There is rarely reason to make a life-and-death choice between people. All should be saved whenever possible. But in the case of an unresolvable conflict, the above scriptural principles indicate the greater good.

In the ordinary discharge of our moral duties to love God and love others, there is usually no conflict. We can love God and self, God and people, the many and the few, the born and the unborn without making painful choices. But moral conflicts not of our own making sometimes arise in our world. When it becomes obvious that you cannot keep two clashing love responsibilities, you must choose the higher over the lower. Thankfully, God has given us His law, the example of His Son, and His abiding Spirit to help us make these choices and fulfill our responsibility to love.

TOUGH QUESTIONS AND STRAIGHT ANSWERS ABOUT VALUE PRINCIPLES

Does the Bible provide value principles that cover biomedical ethics? In other words, are technologies such as artificial insemination, gene splicing, and cloning right or wrong?

Modern technologies that were little more than fantasy fifty years ago have created significant ethical issues in today's world. Artificial insemination, test-tube babies, surrogate mothers, organ transplantation and harvesting, gene splicing, and cloning are all medical realities today. The question is no longer *can* they be done but *should* they be done?

Two opposing views of God and life in our culture provide different answers to the "ought" question and direct us to the loving response in each dilemma.

Judeo-Christian View vs.	Secular Humanism
1. A Creator—God—exists.	1. A Creator—God—does not exist.
2. Humankind was specifically and intentionally created.	2. Humankind evolved from lower forms of life.
3. God is sovereign over all life.	3. Man is sovereign over all life.
4. Sanctity of life is most highly valued.	4. Quality of life is most highly valued.
5. Ends do not necessarily justify means.	5. Ends justify means.

As Christians, we are not categorically opposed to advances in medical technology. But as those who are committed to *serve* God, we view such advances differently than those who by reason of their view seek to *play* God.

The role of the Christian in biomedical issues is to improve human life, not to create it, which is God's prerogative. We prefer genetic fitness but reject genetic fabrication. We strive to cooperate with nature, not to have control over it. As such, assisting an infertile couple through artificial insemination can be good, whereas terminating the life of a fetus because it is genetically less than ideal is wrong. Transplanting an organ from a recently deceased donor preserves life, but growing a fetus expressly for "spare parts" violates the sanctity of life. Experiments to find and eradicate a cancer gene may preserve the lives of countless thousands, but reengineering the gene structure of a fetus to achieve certain physical or mental qualities may violate God's sovereignty in creation. For each conflict we must determine which response preserves and improves human life without usurping God's role as Creator and Sovereign over it. We should use science to *serve* God but never to *play* God.

MATTERS OF LIVING
AND DYING

14

Carlos Velasquez, thirty-one, hovered over his father's hospital bed, searching half-open, vacant eyes for signs of consciousness. Tubes protruded from the older man's nose and mouth. A respirator beside the bed rhythmically breathed for him because the car accident had rendered him comatose and unable to breathe for himself. Carlos had visited his father every day for the past five weeks. The man's condition had not changed. If not for the machine pumping oxygen into his lungs and the IV dripping nutrients into his bloodstream, Mr. Velasquez would be dead.

Greater than the inner pain of seeing his once virile father incapacitated was Carlos's turmoil over what to do for him. The elder Velasquez was only fifty-five years old. Under normal conditions the man would have twenty to thirty more years to enjoy his children and grandchildren. A part of Carlos wanted to do everything possible to keep his father alive until he "woke up" and resumed life. But this was not a normal circumstance. Mr. Velasquez had sustained a severe brain injury, and the doctors offered little hope that the man would regain consciousness let alone resume normal function. Another part of Carlos wanted to say those final words, "Turn off the respirator," and allow his beloved father to rest in peace. The family was divided on the issue, leaving Carlos to make the call. He yearned to know which was the loving choice, life or death.

Perhaps the most difficult challenge facing Christians committed to the love ethic is how to love in matters of living and dying. Is it ever right and loving to intentionally take a human life? Does love ever demand the sacrifice of human beings? What about abortion, mercy killing, suicide, assisted suicide, capital punishment, and war? These are weighty issues. If love does not offer solutions to life-and-death questions like these, it is an unworkable ethic.

YOU SHALL NOT MURDER

The act of intentionally taking an innocent human life is never an act of love as such. "You shall not murder" is in both the Old and New Testaments (Exod. 20:13; Rom. 13:9). The apostle John wrote of murderers, "Their place will be in the fiery lake of burning sulfur. This is the second death" (Rev. 21:8). Peter reminded believers, "If you suffer, it should not be as a murderer" (1 Pet. 4:15). Under the law, those who intentionally took the life of another were to be executed (Exod. 21:23). After Cain killed Abel (Gen. 4:8), murder was rampant through succeeding generations until "the earth was corrupt in God's sight and was full of violence" (Gen. 6:11). God judged the world through the flood.

When Noah and his family emerged from the ark, God commissioned them with these words to enforce the wrongness of murder: "Whoever sheds the blood of man, by man shall his blood be shed; for in the image of God has God made man" (Gen. 9:6). The essential evil of murder is revealed in this passage: Murder is killing God in effigy. Since humankind was created in God's own image, taking a human life is an assault on God. This is why murder was considered worthy of capital punishment.

Even more sobering, murder is not confined to the overt act. Murder can be committed in the heart. Jesus said, "You have heard that it was said to the people long ago, 'Do not murder, and anyone who murders will be subject to judgment.' But I tell you that anyone who is angry with his brother will be subject to judgment" (Matt. 5:21–22). Murder springs from anger rooted in hatred. Jesus said, "From within, out of men's hearts, come evil thoughts, sexual immorality, theft, murder. . . . All these evils come from inside and make a man unclean" (Mark 7:21-23). John flatly declared, "Anyone who hates his brother is a murderer, and you know that no murderer has eternal life in him" (1 John 3:15). Murder at its very root is diametrically opposed to the Christian ethic of love. Murder is hate, and hate is as incompatible with love as darkness is with light.

Love never calls someone to take another life. Hate is unloving just as murder is. Murder is not at all God-like, for God is love. Love demands that we show concern for others, even those who may tempt us to hatred. Jesus commanded, "Love your enemies and pray for those who persecute you" (Matt. 5:44). Paul gave similar instructions: "Do not repay anyone evil for evil. . . . Do not take revenge, my friends, but leave room for God's wrath. . . . On the contrary: 'If your enemy is hungry, feed him; if he is thirsty, give him something to drink.' . . . Do not be overcome by evil, but overcome evil with good" (Rom. 12:17–21). Anger and hatred, which lead to murder in the heart if not the act, are to be replaced by love and good deeds.

However, there are rare occasions when the prohibition against intentionally taking the life of another innocent person is suspended in favor of a higher law, a greater good. For these occasions also God has given us value principles based on His law and Christ's exemplary life, which guide us to the loving thing to do.

SUICIDE AND LIFE SACRIFICING

Taking a life is wrong, even if the life is our own. Suicide is an act of hatred against self just as homicide is an act of hatred against another. Suicide is as wrong as homicide because it violates the command to love self just as murder violates the command to love others. Love is opposed to both. Suicide is a selfish act of terminating our troubles without concern for helping others deal with their troubles. Taking the "easy" way out of life's pain is not the most loving and responsible way out. Love never loses all purpose for living. A person who is focused on protecting and providing for others has no reason to hate his or her own life. Loving is the antidote to the temptation of self-destruction.

Taking a life is unloving, but saving a life is loving. Suicide for selfish reasons is always wrong, but giving up one's life for the sake of saving another is not only acceptable but also commendable. Jesus declared, "Greater love has no one than this, that he lay down his life for his friends" (John 15:13). Christ exemplified the principle of sacrificing one's life for another. He said, "I lay down my life. . . . No one takes it from me, but I lay it down of my own accord" (John 10:17–18). Therefore a scriptural value principle governing our personal lives is: *Suicide is wrong, but sacrificing is justifiable and noble in the loving attempt to save the life of another.*

In the act of pushing a child out of the path of a speeding car, a man is hit and killed. A mother rescues her three-year-old child from drowning in a lake, but drowns in the process. During a drive-by shooting, a young man shields his girlfriend with his own body and dies from gunshot wounds. Two sailors seal themselves inside a flooding compartment to keep the ship from sinking, giving their lives to save the lives of their shipmates. A fighter pilot on a training mission dies by crashing his crippled jet into a vacant field instead of safely ejecting and allowing the aircraft to crash in a residential area. Few of us will have the opportunity to give our lives for another as these people did. But in God's eyes, a life-saving act of self-sacrifice is the highest expression of Christian love, the very antithesis of selfish suicide.

Not every apparent sacrifice of one's life "for others," however, is a true act of love. Paul made this plain in the great love chapter: "If I give all I possess to the poor and surrender my body to the flames, but have not love, I gain nothing" (1 Cor. 13:3). Not every martyr is necessarily dying as an expression of love for others. Some may be sacrificing their lives out of obstinate commitment to their own self-centered cause. There are several examples of selfish suicides in the Bible. Mortally wounded King Saul fell on his own sword to spare himself the shame of dying at the hands of his enemies (1 Sam. 31:4), hardly a loving motive. Abimelech's "assisted suicide" was equally selfish and prideful (Judg. 9:54).

Samson, however, apparently sacrificed his life for unselfish reasons. Just before he caused the temple to collapse on himself and the Philistines, he prayed, "O God, please strengthen me just once more, and let me with one blow get revenge on the Philistines" (Judg. 16:28). God granted his request. Killing more of the enemy in his death than he did in life (v. 30), Samson saved his people from the oppression of the Philistines. *Life sacrifice is only justified when the loving intent is to save other lives.*

The same principle applies when the intent is to rescue people from spiritual death. Christ went to the cross "to give his life as a ransom for many" (Mark 10:45). Paul said he was willing even to give up his spiritual life if it would result in the Jews being saved (Rom. 9:3). In that same spirit of life sacrificing for others, some missionaries risk death from disease when they take the gospel to remote, primitive regions of the world. Christians working in the violent, gang-infested inner city lay their lives on the line to share Christ. Ministers to the poor, to drug addicts, to AIDS patients, and other health risk groups are candidates for life sacrifice.

Whenever we put our lives on the line for the sake of ministry, we are emulating Paul, who said, "I consider my life worth nothing to me, if only I may finish the race and complete the task the Lord Jesus has given me—the task of testifying to the gospel of God's grace" (Acts 20:24). John exhorted us to follow Christ's example: "Jesus Christ laid down his life for us. And we ought to lay down our lives for our brothers" (1 John 3:16).

As rare as life-sacrificing love may be, it is the heart of the Christian love ethic. It is not wrong to die for others; it is the highest act of love one can perform for another human being. Suicide is the ultimate selfish act—*taking* one's life. But life sacrifice is the ultimate selfless act—*giving* one's life for others.

MERCY KILLING AND MERCY DYING

Carlos Velasquez's brain-damaged father is, for all practical purposes, already dead. Is the loving thing to preserve the man's life or let him go? An accident victim is trapped in a fiery mass of tangled metal as a police officer stands by helplessly. Screaming in pain, the victim begs the officer to shoot him and end his torment. Doesn't love demand that he be put out of his misery? An elderly woman, who has suffered episodes of disorientation and memory loss, learns that she has Alzheimer's disease. Years earlier she and her husband had agreed that death with dignity was a greater value to them than life without quality. She asks him to take her to a doctor who is known to provide suicide assistance. Isn't he doing the loving thing to save her from the humiliation and expense of a prolonged and meaningless life?

If it is not loving to take one's own life in suicide, surely it is not loving to help someone else commit suicide. Love demands that the terminally ill be treated with all the mercy possible but not that we take that person's life even at his or her request. Love has a better remedy than life taking to express mercy to the dying. Proverbs 31:6 instructs, "Give beer to those who are perishing, wine to those who are in anguish." In other words, pain-killers, sedatives, and tranquilizers are the merciful, loving response to those dying and in pain, not assisted suicide. Bringing comfort to the dying not only shows mercy but also recognizes the sovereignty of God who said, "I put to death and I bring to life, I have wounded and I will heal, and no one can deliver out of my hand" (Deut. 32:39). The loving God is sovereign over human life. Job said of Him, "The Lord gave and the Lord has taken away; may the name of the Lord be praised" (Job 1:21).

So-called mercy killing and assisted suicide are always unloving, but what about mercy dying—allowing the terminal patient to expire in peace without unnatural and heroic intervention? The Bible does not commit the Christian to perpetuate life as long as possible. Allowing someone to die mercifully and naturally can be a loving alternative, whereas pumping untold dollars and energies into terminal cases can be a most unloving course of action. Our view should be to preserve life, not to prolong death. Injecting medicine to cause or speed death is one thing—and it is morally wrong. But withholding medicine or aids that artificially prolong death is quite another—and is morally right. In brief, mercy killing—no! Mercy dying—yes.

But when do we pull the plug, and who decides? How do we know when a case is terminal? Are not miracles always possible, if not from medical science at least from the hand of God? These are very practical and important questions, and love must weigh the alternatives carefully and responsibly.

When are we justified in allowing someone to die by withholding heroic means? The concept of terminal has two aspects for the Christian. First, it implies that there is no *medical* hope for recovery, as determined by the best medical authorities available. Second, it means that there is no *spiritual* hope for recovery. God has been consulted fervently in prayer according to James 5:13–16 and miraculous recovery has been sought repeatedly (2 Cor. 12:7–9). But when both medical diagnoses and spiritual prospects indicate no hope, and when a margin for error has been duly allowed, love allows life support to be withheld and a natural, painless, merciful death to occur.

Who should decide? It should be a joint decision. The expressed wishes of the dying, the medical wisdom of the physicians, and the counsel of the pastor should all be taken into the final determination by the family. There is greater probability that love will be expressed wisely in a collective decision and less possibility for any one person to bear the psychological guilt that may result. (There is no *moral* guilt because mercy dying under these conditions is the right action.)

The value principle that applies here is: *Taking another life in the name of mercy is unloving, but permitting a terminally ill person to die naturally is merciful and loving.*

LIFE SACRIFICING AND MERCY SACRIFICING

Seven people are adrift in a lifeboat in shark-infested waters. The boat is being swamped from the weight of its load, and if something does not happen soon, all seven will drown or become food for the sharks. Is it right to sacrifice some lives to save the rest? Or, should all be allowed to die? What is the loving thing to do?

Of course, all efforts should be made to save everyone. Perhaps those who are able could take turns in the water, holding on to the boat. But suppose even then the boat will not support everyone. Then, if there are Christians aboard, here is a great opportunity for the self-sacrificing love Christ manifested for us: "Greater love has no one than this, that he lay down his life for his friends" (John 15:13). If there are no volunteers, then the principle of providence can be used. Proverbs says, "The lot is cast into the lap, but its every decision is from the LORD" (16:33). This is how the ancient mariners determined that Jonah should be thrown overboard (Jon. 1:7). And the Bible declares that the lot should be used in weighty matters (Prov. 18:18). Or, all things being equal, it could be determined who in the providence of God were the last to reach the boat. Of course, someone like the captain, whose sea skills may be necessary to save the others, should not be sacrificed. But when "push comes to shove" it is not the loving thing to allow all to perish because of a few who overload the boat.

Consider another example of mercy sacrificing that may come closer to home. A crazy man with an automatic weapon enters a crowded mall and randomly opens fire. In the name of mercy for the many innocent, love may demand the sacrifice of the guilty person. Once all preventative or persuasive methods have been exhausted, shooting to wound or kill the madman before he harms others may be the most loving act.

Occurrences such as these in which mercy sacrificing must be considered are extremely rare, but they illustrate that at times love for others is anything but soft.

LOVE AND CAPITAL PUNISHMENT

Capital punishment, the intentional execution of a guilty person, a murderer, was originally instituted because of a lack of respect for man made in the image of God (Gen. 9:6). It was reinforced in the Mosaic law (Exod. 21:23–25), recognized by Jesus (John 19:11), and restated by Paul when he reminded Christians that the ruler "does not bear the sword for nothing. He is God's servant, an agent of wrath to bring punishment on the wrongdoer" (Rom. 13:4). It is a serious thing to exact capital punishment, so the identity of the murderer must be beyond question and his responsibility for the murder beyond all reasonable doubt.

Capital punishment, when justly administered, is a kind of mercy sacrificing of the guilty for the innocent. Contrary to popular sentiment, capital punishment is not an expression of barbaric disrespect for a murderer's life. It is the murderer who has barbaric disrespect for the worth of human life, not the court that justly sentences him. Love demands that we ask for whom mercy should be shown, the innocent or the guilty. If we fail to insist on justice by the sacrifice of the guilty for the innocent, we show disregard for biblical love and disrespect for the value of an innocent life.

The same justice of God that demanded a substitutionary sacrifice of Christ, life for life, is at the root of the morality of capital punishment. There was no other way to satisfy God's justice than for Christ to give His life for ours (Mark 10:45; 1 Pet. 2:24). And there is no other way to satisfy God's justice and ensure a just and respectful social order than to insist that the life of a murderer be sacrificed. Utter and hateful disregard for the value of individual lives cannot be tolerated by love; love must condemn it. It is loving to value and to protect human life, and capital punishment was instituted to do that very thing. A person's realization that he will lose his life if he takes the life of another will deter most from murder. And one thing is sure: No one who received capital punishment has ever repeated the crime!

LOVE AND ABORTION

The Bible says much about the value of human life. The love principle is clear: You shall not murder. The central issue then is this: Is abortion murder? First, murder must be defined. Murder is the intentional killing of an innocent human being. Thus, the question about abortion can only be answered when the status of the unborn is established. There are three possibilities. First, if the unborn is *fully human*, abortion is murder, and it is wrong in every case except as a sacrifice to save the life of the mother. Second, if the embryo is *prehuman* or *subhuman*— not a person but a thing, then it may be treated like an appendix. No murder is involved in cutting it out. Third, if the unborn is *potentially human* but not fully human, then it must be treated with more respect than a mere thing.

We may safely eliminate the sub-human alternative on biblical grounds. The unborn are the creative work of God, fashioned for human life (Ps. 139:13–18). The unborn are capable of being called by God as Jeremiah was (Jer. 1:5) and filled with the Holy Spirit as John the Baptist was (Luke 1:15, 41). David spoke of himself as being "sinful from the time my mother conceived me" (Ps. 51:5). Things don't sin; only people sin. The unborn are not subhuman entities.

On the other hand, some argue that the unborn are not fully human. But there is neither scientific nor biblical basis for such a conclusion. First, it is scientific fact that a fertilized human ovum is 100 percent human with all genetic characteristics present, including sex. Second, the Bible exacts the same penalty for killing an unborn child as for killing the mother (Exod. 21:22–25). Third, the unborn is called by the same name— "baby"—as the newborn child (Luke 1:41). Fourth, personal pronouns such as *he*, *me*, and *she* are used of the unborn child in Scripture just as they are for other humans (Jer. 1; Ps. 139). Finally, Psalm 139 declares that the unborn are created by God. There is no doubt that the unborn are persons from the moment of conception. They are not potential persons but actual persons with great potential.

The logic is airtight: It is morally wrong to intentionally take the life of an innocent human being; the unborn are innocent human beings; abortion takes the life of innocent unborn human beings; therefore, abortion is morally wrong.

DEFENDING FREEDOM WITH LETHAL FORCE

Another thorny issue faces Christians who are committed to the scriptural love ethic. Does love permit participation in warfare and the killing of military personnel and innocent civilians? Is God's prohibition of murder sometimes suspended for the greater good of love for country and freedom?

God's instruction regarding our relationship to the government is clear. Paul wrote, "Everyone must submit himself to the governing authorities, for there is no authority except that which God has established. The authorities that exist have been established by God. Consequently, he who rebels against the authority is rebelling against what God has instituted, and those who do so will bring judgment on themselves" (Rom. 13:1–2). Peter echoed, "Submit yourselves for the Lord's sake to every authority instituted among men: whether to the king, as the supreme authority, or to governors, who are sent by him to punish those who do wrong and to commend those who do right" (1 Pet. 2:13–14). Do these verses imply that we must obey our government in whatever it commands, even the command to go to war and kill? We cannot give an unconditional yes because, as discussed earlier, the Bible indicates that there are times when love demands disobedience to one's government. Some of the examples bear directly on the command of the government to take lives. The Hebrew midwives refused the king's command to kill newborns (Exod. 1). Obadiah refused Queen Jezebel's command to kill the prophets (1 Kings 18). These cases of disobedience prove that the attitude "my country, right or wrong" is definitely contrary to the principles of love. We are not obligated to always obey the government's command to kill. War is not right simply because a government has decreed it so. We should always obey the government when it takes its place under God but never when it takes the place of God.

Christian love demands selectiveness on the question of war. War is not just simply because our government commands it. On the other hand, war is not wrong simply because our conscience forbids it. Conscience can be wrongly conditioned by culture, sentiment, and expedience (Rom. 2:14, 15; 1 Tim. 4:2). To correct this, conscience should be informed by the realities of life and the responsibility of love.

Selectivism in warfare requires that we understand what constitutes a just war. Not all wars *are* just, therefore we must determine which ones are and which ones are not in order to fulfill our responsibility of love. The value principles discussed in previous chapters are vital to the process of determining if a war is just or unjust. For example, we must ask:

- Is it a war to save many lives at the sacrifice of a few?

- Is it a war against those who disrespect persons in defense of those being held in disrespect?

- Is it a war against those who value economic or territorial gain above human life?

- Is it a war of self-defense against a foreign aggressor?

When the implications of scriptural value principles are applied to contemporary situations, the value principles for a just war emerge.

A just war is declared and fought only by proper authority. Since God instituted government, it is governments alone, not individuals or self-appointed vigilance groups, that have the right to wage war against other governments. We have the right as individuals to protect ourselves against other individuals (Exod. 22:2). But we have no right to fight against our own government. God gave the sword to government for use on the governed (Rom. 13:4), not the other way around. We must submit to authorities and work for necessary reform within proper channels. The children of Israel fled from Pharaoh's oppression; they did not fight him (Exod. 12).

A just war is waged for the protection of the innocent and the deliverance of the oppressed. Abraham went to war against the kings of the valley to rescue his nephew Lot, who had been unjustly captured (Gen. 14). Paul appealed to Rome and accepted military protection from evil men who sought his life (Acts 22, 23). Wars of aggression do not spring from love.

A just war is waged only if all peaceful means for attaining justice fail. The way of love is to seek peace by all reasonable means. Jesus said, "Blessed are the peacemakers" (Matt. 5:9). The Israelites were commanded, "When you march up to attack a city, make its people an offer of peace. . . . If they refuse to make peace and they engage you in battle, lay siege to that city" (Deut. 20:10, 12). Christians are instructed, "If it is possible, as far as it depends on you, live at peace with everyone" (Rom. 12:18); "Make every effort to live in peace with all men" (Heb. 12:14).

A just war is waged with the realistic expectation of victory. A war that has no hope of being successful amounts to no more than a protest that sacrifices more innocent lives to the guilty than no war would have done. The goal of just warfare is to protect the innocent, not sacrifice them unnecessarily. Engaging in a war that cannot be won is mass suicide, and the unnecessary sacrifice of human life is not the loving thing.

A just war is justly waged. God's people in the Old Testament were commanded, "When you lay siege to a city for a long time, fighting against it to capture it, do not destroy its trees by putting an ax to them, because you can eat their fruit. Do not cut them down. . . . However, you may cut down trees that you know are not fruit trees and use them to build siege works until the city at war with you falls" (Deut. 20:19–20). The principle here is to avoid unnecessary destruction, especially of things that are necessary to the continuation of life after the war. The same principle applies to human lives during the war. Nonmilitary personnel should not be military targets.

Love never calls for life taking as such, but it does sometimes call for life sacrificing, mercy dying, mercy sacrificing, capital punishment, and just war. There is only one ground on which love can justify the sacrifice of a human life, and that is the saving of other human lives. Love has the highest regard for human life in all its fullness. Love always insists on the preservation of what is human, even when harsh measures must be taken to attain it.

TOUGH QUESTIONS AND STRAIGHT ANSWERS ON MATTERS OF LIVING AND DYING

Is birth control wrong, since it prohibits human life?

Some Christians believe that deliberately limiting, through contraception, the number of children a woman may bear is a kind of murder in advance. They cite God's sovereignty over life (Gen. 20:18; Deut. 32:39) and claim that birth control is an attempt to play God by controlling life. Yet there is a great difference between preventing life before it starts and taking life after conception, just as there is a difference between a farmer deciding not to plant a certain field and intentionally poisoning recently sprouted crops with lethal herbicide (except, of course, killing a child is murder; killing a crop is not).

Voluntary selectivity with regard to the number of offspring is no more sinful as such than choosing to limit the number of seeds one plants in the yard. In reality, indiscriminate seeding (whether among plants or people) can be more harmful than selective planting. Overcrowding resulting in poverty and ill-health for many is less desirable than intentionally preventing the conception of a few. If limiting through contraception the quantity of people born can enhance the quality of persons living, it is not morally wrong to do so. The method of birth control should, however, not be one that takes the life of a fertilized ovum—that is an abortion—but one that simply prevents conception.

Why did God command Israel to wipe out entire nations, killing men, women, and children? Wasn't Israel's conquest of Canaan a war of aggression?

The Canaanites were far from innocent. Their sins are vividly described in Leviticus 18. God said, "The land was defiled; so I punished it for its sin, and the land vomited out its inhabitants" (v. 25). These people were grossly immoral, stooping even to child sacrifice (v. 21). God had been exceedingly patient with them, declaring to Abraham that He would not allow Israel to conquer the land until the sin of the inhabitants "reached its full measure" (Gen. 15:16)—giving them four hundred years in which to repent! When Israel annihilated the Canaanites, their wickedness deserved utter destruction.

Israel's God-directed attack on the Canaanites was a war of retribution, not aggression. The inhabitants of the Promised

Land had defied and disobeyed their long-suffering Creator to the point of incorrigibility. In response to their incessant rebellion, God finally acted in judgment, removing wickedness from the land and providing a home for His people.

As to the destruction of the innocent children of the Canaanites, several points should be noted. First, with the adult generation entirely polluted by sin, the children, left to themselves, had no chance of avoiding a similar fate. Second, by annihilating the entire population instead of only the adults, God mercifully spared the children a life without parental care and protection. Third, children who die before the age of accountability go to heaven. It was an act of God's mercy to take them into His holy presence from such an unholy environment. Fourth, God is sovereign over life and can order its end according to His will and in view of the person's ultimate good, which is known to Him.

WHEN LOVE DOESN'T HAPPEN

15

Right about now some may be saying, "Josh and Norm, I know you wrote this book to help people like me, but I'm discouraged. I'm not as loving toward God and others as I should be. In fact, I have been indifferent toward some people and downright spiteful toward others at times. And I've been hurt by people who have treated me unkindly or hatefully—even Christian people who are supposed to be loving. I agree with everything you say about love and its importance. But what am I supposed to do when love doesn't happen as it should?"

We understand and share your concern. In reality, there isn't a Christian alive who hasn't felt like a failure at the two great love commandments. So we leave you with a few brief, practical guidelines for dealing with those occasions in life when love doesn't happen the way it should.

WHEN YOU FAIL TO LOVE OTHERS

You've had a killer day and walk in the front door wound tighter than a coiled spring. Instead of greeting you cheerfully, the kids instantly start whining and poking one another and demanding their supper. You lose it in a big way. "Go to your rooms and leave me alone!" you snap angrily. They slink away deflated and in tears.

The lunch room conversation degenerates to a chop session aimed at the boss, except the boss isn't there to defend himself. Encouraged by your coworkers' boldness, you put in your two cents' worth, saying some unkind things you know are only partially true.

Your neighbor has cancer and only a few months to live. You know you should get over to visit her, offer to help her, and share Christ with her. But you're so busy with your own life that you keep putting it off. Before you know it, she's gone—and you never went to visit as you intended.

What do you do when you realize that you blew it, that you spoke or acted in an unloving manner toward people and, in so doing, toward God? Instead of berating yourself or questioning God's presence in your life, quickly take these steps and resume your growth as a loving person.

Confess your sin to God and receive His forgiveness. Several years ago I (Josh) succumbed to a bad case of lead foot and received a speeding ticket for going 85 miles per hour. When I went in to pay the stiff fine, the clerk said, "If you take a three-hour safe-driving class, you won't have to pay the fine." I took the class and received a notice of completion from the instructor. When I presented the slip to the court clerk, she said, "Your record is wiped clean." As I drove home that day, I thought,

What a beautiful illustration of what Christ did with my sins. I was totally guilty, but He wiped the slate clean at the cross.

Jesus Christ paid the price for all our unloving words and deeds. When we confess our unloving words and deeds, it is God's nature to forgive the penitent sinner. Exodus 34:6, 7 tells us that He is a "compassionate and gracious God, slow to anger, abounding in love and faithfulness, . . . forgiving wickedness, rebellion and sin." Paul wrote, "[God] has rescued us from the dominion of darkness and brought us into the kingdom of the Son he loves, in whom we have redemption, the forgiveness of sins" (Col. 1:13, 14).

Our responsibility is to confess our failure to love others and receive God's forgiveness according to 1 John 1:9: "If we confess our sins, he is faithful and just and will forgive us our sins and purify us from all unrighteousness." Confession and forgiveness can happen in a moment's time. Once you realize you have blown it, go to God immediately and say, "I blew it, I didn't love as I should." If God were to respond verbally to your confession, He might say something like, "Yes, you blew it. But because you have trusted My Son and have confessed your sin, you are forgiven, your record has been wiped clean." The psalmist promises us, "As far as the east is from the west, so far has he removed our transgressions from us" (Ps. 103:12). And that includes every unloving or selfish deed we confess to Him.

Forgive yourself. It's amazing how some Christians can confess their sin and thank God for His forgiveness is one breath then turn around and berate themselves for their failure in the next. "What a dumb thing to do. How could you have said such an unloving thing? You're a sorry excuse for a Christian. How can God ever use you after what you did? You had better get your act together."

It's crazy to accept the death of Christ as the basis for God's forgiveness and then think you have to get down on yourself or do better in order to let yourself off the hook. Not only is it illogical, it is also dishonoring to God. It's like saying His sacrifice satisfied Him, but it wasn't good enough to satisfy you when you blow it. Stop beating yourself up for your failures; Christ has already taken the beating for you. Acknowledge the sufficiency of God's forgiveness by forgiving yourself.

Make things right where you can. If your last words before turning out the light were insensitive, angry, or hurtful, quietly confess your sin to God, then apologize to your spouse before you both fall asleep, asking for forgiveness. If you ignored your son's plea for help with his homework because you were "too busy" watching TV, confess it, turn the TV off, apologize to him, and see what you can do to help him. Whether you have offended a family member, friend, coworker, neighbor, fellow church member, or stranger, make every effort to admit your fault and seek their forgiveness. If your offense has cost the person money or damaged property, be prepared to make restitution. Or if your unloving words of gossip have unleashed rumors about someone, make every effort to squelch those rumors and set the record straight with everyone involved.

Whenever possible, speak in person to the one you have offended, acknowledging your unloving behavior and asking for forgiveness. If meeting him or her face to face is not convenient, make a telephone call, send a memo, or write a letter. It is important to do everything within your power to make things right just as soon as you realize that you have been selfish or unloving toward someone. If you have offended someone with whom you have lost touch, ask God to bring that person across your path in person or by phone or letter so you can resolve the offense.

Be aware that not everyone will accept your apology and forgive you for being unloving. While in a restaurant once, I (Josh) said something out of line in the hearing of a Christian brother. I didn't realize how awful it was until I was driving home and the Holy Spirit convicted me of my sin. I confessed it to God, then I turned around and went back to the restaurant. When I found the man, I said, "What I said tonight was wrong. I apologize for being so unloving. Will you forgive me?"

He said, "No, I won't forgive you. You never should have said it." Stunned, I replied, "I agree with you wholeheartedly. I never should have said it, but I did and I'm sorry. Will you forgive me?" Again he refused. We went back and forth on the issue for several minutes, but he wouldn't budge. I left the restaurant forgiven by God but unforgiven by the man I had offended.

I had a pity party for about forty-five minutes, raking myself over the coals and blaming myself for the man's obstinacy. Then I thought, *This is ridiculous. I confessed my sin to God and He has forgiven me. I have apologized as lovingly as I know how. If he can't forgive me, that's too bad, but it's his problem, not mine.* I threw my shoulders back and changed my attitude right then and there.

If you wait for the offended person to forgive you before you forgive yourself, you are shifting the basis of forgiveness from Christ's sacrifice to the attitude of the person you offended. If you sincerely apologize for your unloving words or deeds but get the same treatment I did in that restaurant, don't hold a grudge against the person or get down on yourself. Let it go. Let God deal with the unforgiving person. You have done your part.

WHEN OTHERS FAIL TO LOVE YOU

Even the most loving, kind people in your world are capable of unloving words and deeds. At one time or another you may feel the sting of a coworker's grudge, a parent's broken promise, a spouse's unfaithfulness, a friend's careless words, a child's unkind act, or a stranger's resentment. How should you respond when someone breaks the law of love and you are the victim of those words or deeds?

You must respond as the man in the restaurant would not: You must forgive. Forgiveness is a conscious decision to wipe the slate clean of all judgment, to give up all resentment, to release the offender from the debt of his or her act, and personally accept the price of reconciliation.

Forgiveness is clearly a command, not a suggestion, for the Christian. Jesus said, "When you stand praying, if you hold anything against anyone, forgive him, so that your Father in heaven may forgive you your sins" (Mark 11:25); "If you forgive men when they sin against you, your heavenly Father will also forgive you. But if you do not forgive men their sins, your Father will not forgive your sins" (Matt. 6:14–15). Paul echoed Christ's command: "Be kind and compassionate to one another, forgiving each other, just as in Christ God forgave you" (Eph. 4:32); "Clothe yourselves with compassion, kindness, humility, gentleness and patience. Bear with each other and forgive whatever grievances you may have against one another. Forgive as the Lord forgave you" (Col. 3:12–13). Since we have been forgiven by God, we cannot withhold forgiveness from others, as Jesus illustrated in the parable of the unjust servant in Matthew 18:23–35.

Consider a few cautions about forgiveness. First, forgiveness is not a feeling. If you wait until you feel like forgiving the hurt you have suffered, you may never forgive. Forgiveness is a conscious decision to wipe the slate clean in spite of the pain you may have suffered.

Second, forgiveness does not mean pretending the offense never happened, condoning the wrong done to you, or demanding that your offender change his behavior. If the person is doing something morally or legally wrong or hurtful, he should be confronted and held accountable for his actions. But we are to forgive whether or not the offender changes.

Third, forgiveness is not the same as forgetting. You can completely forgive someone and still remember the offense. Hopefully, over time, the memory will fade. But it is certain that you will never forget the offense if you don't first forgive.

You may wonder, "If forgiveness is vital to the biblical love ethic, why are Christians often so reticent to forgive those who offend them?" There are several reasons we don't forgive:

- We like feeling superior to someone else. But instead of looking for something to criticize or gloat over in others, we are to focus on that which is good and positive in them (Phil. 4:8).

- We sometimes enjoy harboring a grudge and "rubbing it in." But we are commanded to get rid of all bitterness because it grieves the Holy Spirit (Eph. 4:30–32).

- We can't get past the anger. Yet Paul warns, "'In your anger do not sin': Do not let the sun go down while you are still angry" (Eph. 4:26).

- We expect to be hurt again. That is putting limits on forgiveness instead of forgiving limitlessly as Christ commanded (Matt. 18:21, 22). It is keeping score of wrongs suffered, something love doesn't do (1 Cor. 13:5).

- We are filled with self-pity. "Woe is me, I've been so hurt, and I don't deserve it," we moan. Instead, we must rejoice that God can bring good out of all things—even the unloving words or deeds of others (Rom. 8:28).

Forgiveness is an expression of love, and love takes the initiative to forgive, even if the offender does not ask for forgiveness. In being eager forgivers, we are following God's example; He extended forgiveness to us before we even knew we had sinned: "God demonstrates his own love for us in this: While we were still sinners, Christ died for us" (Rom. 5:8); "This is love: not that we loved God, but that he loved us and sent his Son as an atoning sacrifice for our sins" (1 John 4:10). We should imitate God's willingness to forgive quickly and fully.

We must also be ready to forgive repeatedly those who offend us repeatedly. In Christ's time, the consensus among the rabbis was that a person should be forgiven up to four times for the same offense. Some of the more generous teachers would forgive as many as seven times. That's why Peter asked Jesus, "Lord, how many times shall I forgive my brother when he sins against me? Up to seven times?" (Matt. 18:21). Jesus' answer showed that our forgiveness should have no bounds: "I tell you, not seven times, but seventy-seven times" (v. 22). We must forgive every offense and every offender every time.

THE POWER TO FORGIVE

If you are beginning to think forgiveness can be difficult, you're right. Where do we find the power to forgive when we are tempted instead to harbor a grudge, seek revenge, or flaunt our superiority? The power comes from God, the great forgiver.

First, you can forgive because you have the provision and example of Jesus Christ. Forgiveness was an integral part of Christ's earthly ministry, extending even to the men who crucified Him (Luke 23:34). His sacrifice on the cross provided for your forgiveness and is the basis for forgiving others. Study the example of Christ's life and acknowledge that His death is your basis for forgiving any and all offenses you suffer.

Second, you can forgive because you have the indwelling presence of the Holy Spirit. You are not in this alone. God lives within you to work out His good purposes in your life (Phil. 2:13). Be continually filled with the Holy Spirit and trust Him to energize you to forgive.

Third, you can forgive because you have the guidance of God's Word. Saturate yourself with the Scriptures about love cited in this book. Memorize them. Meditate on them. As the Word of God becomes deeply rooted in your heart and mind, you will find yourself willing and able to obey it (Col. 3:16).

Finally, you can forgive because you have the power of prayer at your disposal. Make this prayer a part of your daily communication with God: "Heavenly Father, thank You for sending Jesus Christ to die on the cross that I might be totally forgiven for my sins. Help me to quickly confess my unloving words and acts today. Give me the strength to swallow my pride and seek the forgiveness of others when I have been unloving. Show me how to forgive myself and take the initiative to forgive those who are unloving toward me. I ask for conviction when I need conviction, healing when I need healing, and comfort when I need comfort. Let me be a channel of Your love and forgiveness to the world today."

Chapter 2

1. Josh McDowell and Bob Hostetler, *Right from Wrong* (Dallas, Word Publishing, 1995), p. 81, 82.

Chapter 4

1. Quoted in Max Anders, *30 Days to Under-standing the Bible* (Dallas: Word Publishing, 1994), p. 120.

Chapter 6

1. C.S. Lewis, *The Four Loves* (New York: Harcourt Brace Jovanovich, 1960), p. 134.
2. Ibid., p. 98
3. Ibid., pp. 91, 92.
4. Ibid., p. 176
5. Ibid., p. 177

Chapter 7

1. C.S. Lewis, *The Four Loves*, pp. 13, 14.
2. Ibid., pp. 177, 178.